Cooking with Grandma and the Girls

Cooking

with

Grandma

and the

Girls

Yesterday's Recipes for Today's Lifestyles

by
Brenda Shriver

Tapestry Press
Irving, Texas

DE

Tapestry Press
3649 Conflans Road
Suite 103
Irving, TX 75061

Printed in the United States of America

05 04 03 02 01 5 4 3 2 1

Library of Congress Cataloging-in-Publication Data
    Shriver, Brenda, 1941-
    Cooking with grandma and the girls : yesterday's recipes for today's
lifestyles / by Brenda Shriver.
        p. cm.
    Includes index.
    ISBN 1-930819-06-4 (Trade paper : alk. paper)
    1. Cookery, American. I. Title.
    TX715 .S6635 2001
                        641.5973—dc21 2001005646

Images of recipe cards are property of the author. All other images are copyright © by
www.arttoday.com or by Corel Corporation and are used by permission.

Book design and layout by
D. & F. Scott Publishing, Inc.
North Richland Hills, Texas

Cover design by David Sims

Nutrition data by Carole Fong Kutchins, M.S., R.D., L.D. and Brenda Shriver

This book is dedicated to
Sara Elnora Shriver
Oma Jackson Day
and all the other grandmothers
who passed along these recipes
and the love of cooking.

Contents

Contents

Contents

Contents

Yesterday's Recipes for Today's Lifestyles

Since I love to cook and have written several cookbooks, I was fortunate enough to inherit the wonderful collection of my mother-in-law, Sara Elnora Shriver's, (otherwise known as Eleanor) recipes and cookbooks. In exchange for this marvelous collection, I was asked to compile the family favorites into a cookbook and make copies for each of my husband's siblings. The original intent was to use only Mom Shriver's recipes, but as I was researching the various recipes, I realized many of the recipes were from her neighbors, family or friends from the different organizations she had belonged to. Probably the most long-standing group was a sewing group she had belonged to since my husband, John, was a baby, they called themselves "the gang" or "the girls." With these friends in mind, I knew it would have to be more than "Grandma's Cookbook." I would have to include "the girl's" recipes as well. Next I started to think of all the wonderful old recipes from my mom, which I would also like to include, thus the title *Cooking with Grandma and the Girls*.

These recipes are not something they tore out of the paper, nor are they typed neatly. For the most, part the recipes are written out in their own handwriting. Some of these recipes have been handed down from generation to generation by word of mouth, in small tattered notebooks, or on scraps of paper. They are a story of their lives and as such, a history worth saving. Each cook knew exactly what proportions to add by pinches and dabs, they knew how to "sugar to sweeten" or how much was "enough flour to make stiff." Most of these ladies were such good cooks, all they needed was a general idea of the ingredients and they knew what to do from there on. This is the reason for all the vague instructions on some of these old recipes, or even worse, no instructions at all. As I was trying to standardize these original recipes, I realized most of them were very high in fat, calories, sodium, etc. Being a champion of healthy eating, I was challenged to make these family recipes more in keeping with our healthier style of eating. I was intrigued with the challenge, so I thought, "why not give it a try"! Off to the kitchen I went, adding, subtracting, and substituting ingredients. I spent countless hours compiling and then testing, until I finally had a compilation of recipes I am very pleased with. Out of these thoughts came the seeds of a dream for a new cookbook, *Cooking with Grandma and the Girls: Yesterday's Recipes for Today's Lifestyles*.

In this book, I have presented the old favorites in their original form—misspelled words and all. I felt the original recipes held such charm that I wanted to share them with you, my readers. While I have revised most of these recipes for a healthier version of that particular recipe, I have also included several recipes without a revision. In attempting to create healthier versions of these recipes, I came to the conclusion, "there are some things just too delicious to tamper with." To mention just a few of the recipes I was thinking of; graham cracker cream pie, lazy daisy cake, rump roast and poteca, Aunt Bess's wonderful nut roll bread. I have also included several charts to help you work out your old recipes. On the light side, I have included a few poems which could have come from Grandma and the girls, but in fact they are just poems I have collected over the years and the authors are unknown.

I hope you enjoy the recipes, as well as the "precious memories" from our friends and family that I have shared with you. It is my hope that these recipes can be preserved for future generations in their original form and that you will save them for the times when you make the decision to splurge on a special treat. I hope that at other times you will use the revised versions when you want comfort food with a taste of grandma's cooking.

If I Had My Life to Live Over

I'd dare to make more mistakes next time, I'd relax, I'd limber up, and I'd be sillier than I have been in this life time. I'd take fewer things seriously, I'd take more chances, and I'd climb more mountains and swim more rivers. I'd eat more ice cream and less vegetables. I would perhaps have more actual troubles, but I'd have a fewer imaginary ones.

You see, I'm one of those people who live sensibly hour after hour, day after day. Oh, I've had my moments, and if I had it to do over again, I'd have more of them. In fact, I'd try to have nothing else. Just moments, one after another instead of living so many years ahead of each day. I've been one of those persons who never goes anywhere without thermometer, raincoat, umbrella. and aspirin. If I had it to do over again, I'd travel lighter than I have.

If I had my life to live over, I'd start going barefoot earlier in the spring and stay that way later in the fall. I'd go to more dances. I'd ride more merry-go-rounds. I'd pick more daisies.

Author unknown

Helpful Information

Helpful Information

As I researched hundreds of old recipes, it was very obvious many of them did not have the specific instructions we appreciate today; such as temperature, pan size, or cooking time, and their can sizes were listed differently from today. I have listed some equivalents I hope will help you in working out some of your "Grandma's recipes."

Cooking Temperatures

In Grandma's days all of her cooking would be done over an open fire or a stove heated by coal or wood. Our Grandma's did not have the luxury of simply turning a dial to heat and determine the temperature of her stove. She would judge the temperature by how long she could hold her hand over the range or in the oven. If she could hold her hand in the oven for 60 seconds that was a slow oven, 30 seconds = moderate; 20 seconds = hot; 15 seconds = very hot; and 5 seconds = extremely hot. Below I have listed their equivalents.

Slow oven = 250–300 degrees
Moderately slow = 300–325 degrees
Moderate = 350 degrees
Moderately hot = 375 degrees
Hot = 400–425 degrees
Very hot = 425–475 degrees
Extremely hot = 475–525 degrees

Can Equivalents:

Because so many of the older recipes call for cans by the number, such as #2 can, etc. this will be a helpful chart as you follow your Grandma's recipes.

#300 can = 1¾ cups
#303 can = 2 cups
#2 can = 2½ cups
#2½ can = 3½ cups
#3 can = 5¾ cups
#10 can = 12–13 cups

Helpful Info

Terms in Grandma's Recipes

A dab is about 1 teaspoon
A pinch is less than a dab
A lump is the size of an egg
A small lump is the size of a walnut
Sprinkle means several shakes
Crumble means the size of peas
Well done varies
To taste means not too much or not too little
Heaping means running over
Scant means not quite full
                Author unknown

Today's Standard Measurements:

3 teaspoons = 1 tablespoon
2 tablespoons = ⅛ cup
4 tablespoons = ¼ cup
5 tablespoons + 1 teaspoon = ⅓ cup
1 jigger = 3 tablespoons
½ cup + 2 tablespoons = ⅝ cup
¾ cup + 2 tablespoons = ⅞ cup
1 oz. = 2 tablespoons fat or liquid
4 oz. = ½ cup
16 oz. = 1 lb.
2 cups = 1 pint
4 cups = 1 quart
4 quarts = 1 gallon
1 pint = 1 lb.
1 gill liquid = ½ cup
2 cups granulated sugar = 1 lb.
3½ cups powdered sugar = 1 lb.
2¼ cup brown sugar = 1 lb.
4 cups sifted all-purpose flour = 1 lb.
2 cups butter or margarine = 1 lb.
A few grains = less then ⅛ teaspoon
Pinch = as much as can be taken between the tips of finger and thumb
Speck = less than a pinch
Walnut size lump of butter = 2 tablespoons
Butter the size of Hen's egg = 3 tablespoons

Helpful Cooking Definitions:

Bake: To cook by dry heat in an oven

Barbecue: To roast slowly on a gridiron, spit, over coals, or under a free flame or oven electric unit, usually basting with a highly seasoned sauce.

Beat: To whip with a spoon or beater in order to combine food or introduce air into the mixture.

Blend: To mix two or more ingredients thoroughly.

Boil: To cook at boiling temperature

Braise: To cook by direct heat

Chop: To cut coarsely with a knife or cleaver

Cream: To work one or more foods until soft and creamy

Cube: To cut into small even pieces

Dice: To cut into cubes, about ¼ inch in size

Dredge: To dip in or sprinkle with flour

Fold: To combine ingredients by blending with a spoon or whisk, using an up-and-over motion.

Fricassee: To cook by braising; usually applied to fowl, rabbit, or veal cut into pieces

Fry: To cook in fat

Knead: To manipulate with a pressing motion plus folding and stretching

Marinate: To let set in a mixture of oil and vinegar, lemon juice, or some other marinade

Mix: To combine ingredients in any way

Parbroil: To partially cook in water

Poach: To cook in water just below the boiling point

Pot Roast: To cook slowly by moist heat

Roast: To cook by dry heat in the oven

Sauté: To cook in a small amount of fat

Sear: To brown quickly

Simmer: To cook by moist heat at a low temperature

Singe: To burn the hair off poultry

Steam: To cook in steam with or without pressure

Steep: To allow a substance to stand in liquid below the boiling point for the purpose of extracting flavor or color

Stew: To cook slowly in liquid

Truss: To fasten together with string or skewers

Whip: To beat rapidly to produce expansion

Breads and Breakfast

Breads and Breakfast

M y mom never followed a recipe for making biscuits, corn bread, or many other things. Consequently, as I became more interested in cooking I would follow her around the kitchen as she cooked, measuring ingredients before she combined them. In this way, I was able to capture some of her recipes in terms of standardized measurements instead of dabs and pinches.

Baking Powder Biscuits

3 cups flour
1 teaspoon salt
4 teaspoons baking powder
6 tablespoons shortening
1 cup sweet milk

Sift flour, baking powder and salt. Cut in shortening, add milk. Turn out onto lightly floured board; knead slightly. Roll out, cut with floured cutter. Bake in hot oven 450 degrees, 12 minutes or until brown.
Makes about 24

Cal	Prot	Fat	Carb	Fiber	Chol	Sodium
92kc	1g	3g	12g	0g	3mg	184mg

Biscuits (Revised)

2 cups reduced-fat baking mix
¾ cup reduced-fat milk

While these biscuits may not be quite as light and flaky as my mom's biscuits, they are considerably lower in fat with the added benefit of being quick and easy to make.

Heat oven to 450 degrees; lightly spray baking sheet with vegetable spray. Stir milk into baking mix until soft dough forms.
Rolled biscuits: Turn onto lightly floured surface, knead slightly. Roll out, cut with floured cutter.
Drop biscuits: Drop dough by tablespoonfuls onto prepared baking sheet.
Bake in 450 degree oven for 7–9 minutes or until browned.

Yield: twelve 2″ biscuits

Cal	Prot	Fat	Carb	Fiber	Chol	Sodium
120kc	6.6g	.8g	22.7g	<1g	.4mg	365mg

Sandwich Buns

Put to heat 2 cups run over, milk
1 cup water, make hot but don't boil. Meanwhile put ½ cake yeast and 1 tblsp sugar in one cup real warm water. Mix ½ cup shortening, ½ cup sugar, 1 tblsp salt together. Pour in hot milk then add yeast. Add flour 'til stiff and sticky but won't stick to hand, about 10–12 cups.
Let rise 2–3 hours, work down. Let rise 2 hours, make into buns. Let rise about 1½ to 2 hours
Bake 375 degree about 35 minutes or until brown, grease buns with Crisco and a brush. Makes about 45 buns

Recipe from: Isabelle Shriver Smail

Cal	Prot	Fat	Carb	Fiber	Chol	Sodium
124kc	3g	3g	21g	0g	2mg	153mg

Basic Roll Dough

1 pkg. active dry yeast
¼ cup warm water
1 cup milk, scalded
¼ cup sugar
¼ cup melted shortening or
 margarine
1 egg
1 teaspoon salt
3½ cups all-purpose flour

Isabelle's recipe is delicious, but tricky to follow instructions. I find the following recipe to be similar to the recipe my mother always used for holidays and much easier to follow.

Soften yeast in warm water (110 degrees), let stand 5 minutes. Combine milk, sugar, shortening, egg, and salt; cool to lukewarm. Add 1½ cups flour to warm milk mixture, beat well. Beat in yeast; gradually add remaining flour until it forms a soft dough. Knead 8–10 minutes, or until smooth and elastic. Place in greased bowl turning once to grease surface; cover and let rise until double, about 1½ to 2 hours.*

Turn out on lightly floured surface and shape as desired. Place rolls on greased baking sheets; cover and let shaped rolls rise until doubled, 35–45 minutes. Bake in hot oven 400 degrees for 12–14 minutes. Brush with butter last couple of minutes if desired.

Yield: 36 rolls sandwich buns

*Dough can be refrigerated while rising, it will take 2–12 hours.

Cal	Prot	Fat	Carb	Fiber	Chol	Sodium
74kc	2g	2g	11g	0g	8mg	68mg

Breads and Breakfast

I can still picture my mom, a short, stout lady, moving around the kitchen preparing our family's favorite foods, humming or singing a hymn as she worked. Mom, having been a Christian since she was a young girl, loved to sing the old hymns and especially as she worked around the house. A few of her favorites were: "How Great Thou Art," "Old Rugged Cross," and "Nearer My God To Thee." I only need to hear one of these old hymns to bring tears to my eyes and the picture (with sound) of her singing and cooking as she moved about her domain.

Mom came from a background where so much of the food was fried, and there is nothing better for frying food than an iron skillet. She had a wonderful collection of iron skillets and griddles in various sizes and was adamant about certain foods being cooked in the iron skillets. Corn bread is just one example and I heartily agree with her, there is no comparison between cooking corn bread in the skillet and cooking it in a glass or aluminum baking pan. Pouring the corn bread batter into a hot greased skillet gives it such a nice crispy, brown crust which you don't get in other baking pans. If you are fortunate enough to have iron skillets I have included some tips on caring for them on page 237.

Corn Bread

1 egg
1 cup lard or shortening
½ cup sugar
1 cup butter milk
1 cup corn meal
2 cups flour
1 teaspoon soda
salt

Melt lard in iron skillet. Mix everything together, add most of the melted lard, and beat well. Pour into the hot greased skillet and bake in a hot oven till done.

Cal	Prot	Fat	Carb	Fiber	Chol	Sodium
58kc	1g	8g	6g	0g	3mg	51mg

Corn Bread (Revised)

Preheat oven to 425 degrees; spray a 9″ iron skillet, 8″ square pan or 12 cup muffin tin with vegetable spray, (if using an iron skillet heat after spraying, before adding batter). Combine meal, flour, sugar, baking powder and salt; add milk and egg. Beat with spoon until smooth. Pour into hot greased skillet or prepared baking pan. Bake in 425 degree oven for 20–25 minutes.

Yield: 8 servings

vegetable spray
1¼ cup yellow corn meal
¾ cup all-purpose flour
¼ cup sugar, or less, optional
4 teaspoons baking powder
½ teaspoon salt
1 cup reduced-fat milk
1 egg or 2 egg whites

Cal	Prot	Fat	Carb	Fiber	Chol	Sodium
170kc	5g	1.5g	34g	2g	25mg	410mg

Breads and Breakfast

Hot Cakes

1 egg, beaten
1 cup milk
1 cup flour
4 teaspoons baking powder
½ teaspoon salt
2 tablespoons melted butter

Sift flour, baking powder and salt together; add egg, milk, and butter. Cook on hot griddle till done.

Cal	Prot	Fat	Carb	Fiber	Chol	Sodium
110kc	4g	4g	14g	0g	35mg	440mg

Hot Cakes (Revised)

In a medium bowl combine flour, baking powder and salt; in a small bowl combine egg, milk, and butter. Using a wire whisk add liquids to flour mixture, beat until smooth. Heat griddle or nonstick skillet, spray lightly with vegetable spray. When hot, pour about ¼ cup batter onto prepared griddle. Cook until top surface bubbles, turn once; cook until brown on underside. Serve immediately.

1 cup all-purpose flour
4 teaspoons baking powder
dash salt
1 egg, beaten
1 cup + 2 tablespoons
    reduced-fat milk
1 tablespoon melted margarine
vegetable spray

Yield: eight 3–4″ hot cakes

Cal	Prot	Fat	Carb	Fiber	Chol	Sodium
90kc	3g	2.5g	14g	0g	25mg	290mg

Breads & Breakfast

Irish Soda Bread

6 cups all-purpose flour
1 tablespoon baking powder
1½ teaspoon baking soda
2 teaspoon salt
¼ cup sugar
2½ cups buttermilk
2 tablespoon margarine
1½ cups raisins

Combine flour, baking powder, soda, salt, and sugar; set aside. Combine buttermilk, margarine and raisins, add to flour mixture; stir until moistened. Knead on floured surface about 5 minutes or until smooth. Place on greased cookie sheet and press into a circle about 1½" thick. Bake at 325 degrees for 1 hour or until breads sounds hollow when tapped. Cool slightly before serving.

Yield: 12 servings

Recipe from: Angela Ciochetti Shriver

Cal	Prot	Fat	Carb	Fiber	Chol	Sodium
340kc	9g	3g	71g	3g	0mg	750mg

Breads and Breakfast

Pumpkin Bread

3⅓ cups flour
2 teaspoons soda
3 cups sugar
1½ teaspoons salt
1 teaspoon cinnamon
1 teaspoon nutmeg
Mix and add:
1 cup oil
4 eggs, beaten
⅔ cup water
2 cups pumpkin

Mix all ingredients in electric mixer. Bake 1 to 1½ hours at 350 degrees in greased angel food cake pan.

Cal	Prot	Fat	Carb	Fiber	Chol	Sodium
210kc	2g	8g	33g	2g	25mg	230mg

Recipe from: Joyce Osborne

Pumpkin Bread (Revised)

Preheat oven to 350 degrees; spray a tube pan, or two 4×8 loaf pans with vegetable spray.

Combine flour, soda, baking powder, salt, cinnamon, and nutmeg; set aside. In a mixing bowl combine oil, apple sauce, and sugar; add eggs, beating well after each addition; stir in pumpkin. Gradually add flour mixture, alternating with water, beat well. Pour into prepared pans, bake 1½ hours for tube pans, bake 70–75 minutes for loaf pans; or until wooden pick comes out clean. Cool 10 minutes in pan before inverting, turn out onto rack to cool.

Yield: 32 slices

3⅓ cups all-purpose flour
2 teaspoon baking soda
½ teaspoon baking powder
¼ teaspoon salt
1 teaspoon cinnamon
1 teaspoon nutmeg
¾ cup vegetable oil
¼ cup applesauce
3 cups sugar
2 eggs, + 3 egg whites, beaten
2 cups cooked pumpkin
⅔ cup water

Cal	Prot	Fat	Carb	Fiber	Chol	Sodium
190kc	2g	6g	33g	2g	10mg	140mg

Poteca
(Nut Roll Bread)

This recipe came from Aunt Bess VonHoff, who was John's aunt on his dad's side. This recipe for nut roll bread falls into the group of recipes that I mentioned earlier, which is just too delicious to change. Make it for special occasions and enjoy smaller portions of it.

The directions may look complicated, but they really are not. As with all yeast breads, they take time to make from beginning to end. However, so much of the time is spent in the dough raising, you can be about your own business.

(Comments within parentheses are mine.)

4 cups flour
1½ teaspoon salt
3 tablespoons sugar
½ lb. butter (room
    temperature)
1 cake yeast*
1 teaspoon sugar
¼ cup lukewarm water
3 egg yolks, beaten
1 cup lukewarm milk

Heat ¼ cup water to 85 degrees, dissolve 1 teaspoon sugar and 1 cake of yeast in hot water; it will be foamy, let rest for 10 minutes. While yeast is resting: Measure flour, add salt and sugar. Cut in butter, work into crumbs. Combine lukewarm milk, egg yolks, and yeast mixture. Make a dent in flour and butter mixture, pour liquids and eggs in; stir to blend thoroughly. Sprinkle flour on a board and knead 5–10 minutes, until nice and smooth and elastic. Put dough in greased bowl and grease top of dough; cover with wax paper and cloth, let raise until double in bulk or cover and let stand overnight in ice box (refrigerator).

(Aunt Bess rolled all the dough at one time, using a large piece of muslin that enabled her to actually roll the dough into a roll.)

In the morning, roll or pull dough on floured cloth until it measures 27 by 30 inches. Spoon filling mixture** onto dough, spread to within 1″ of edge; roll jellyroll fashion. Lift roll onto greased baking sheet; cover and let stand about 30 minutes. (Aunt Bess would position her baking sheet next to the nut roll, she would lift one end of the roll onto baking sheet then flip the other end, shaping in a U shape, or you could just cut the roll in 2 or 3 different sections. I found it easier to divide the dough into four portions and make four separate rolls.) Preheat oven to 375 degrees, bake bread 10 minutes, reduce heat to 350 and continue to bake about 30 minutes more, or until bread sounds hollow when tapped and is nicely browned.

Yield: four 15″ long rolls or approximately sixty 1″ slices

*Can use 1 pkg. dry yeast.
**See page 17 for filling.

Nutrition data for dough only

Cal	Prot	Fat	Carb	Fiber	Chol	Sodium
70kc	1g	3.5g	7g	0g	20mg	90mg

Nut Filling for Poteca

2 lb. groundnuts
½ cup butter, melted
1 cup milk, scalded
4 egg whites, beaten stiff
1 cup sugar

Pour milk over melted butter and nuts; stir. Add sugar and beaten egg whites. Mix well and spread over dough.

Cal	Prot	Fat	Carb	Fiber	Chol	Sodium
120kc	4g	10g	5g	<1g	5mg	20mg

Yield: 60 servings

Recipe from: Elaine VonHoff Federico, Aunt Bess's daughter

Poppy Seed Filling

Mix all ingredients well before spreading over dough.

Yield: 60 servings

1½ cups ground poppy seeds
1 cup sugar
½ cup scalded milk

Cal	Prot	Fat	Carb	Fiber	Chol	Sodium
32kc	0g	1g	4g	0g	0mg	2mg

Nut & Poppy Seed Filling

This is my favorite filling; I usually make half the nut-filling recipe for half the dough, and then make half of the following recipe, using poppy seeds and nuts as well.

Melt butter, about ¼ cup, spread over dough. Take about 1 cup sugar, sprinkle over dough and sprinkle poppy seeds over as thick as you want. Take cinnamon and shake over dough. Roll up jellyroll fashion; leave stand about 30 minutes. You can add chopped nuts with it if you like.

Yield: 60 servings

Recipes from: Elaine VonHoff Federico, Aunt Bess's daughter

Cal	Prot	Fat	Carb	Fiber	Chol	Sodium
54kc	0g	4g	4g	0g	0mg	24mg

Breads & Breakfast

Grandma's Bananna (sic) Nut Bread

2 cups sifted flour
½ cup Spry
3 banannas, (sic) mashed
1 tsp. soda
1 cup sugar
2 eggs
1 cup chopped walnuts

(There were no directions with this recipe.)

Cal	Prot	Fat	Carb	Fiber	Chol	Sodium
200kc	4g	9g	30g	1g	25mg	180mg

Recipe from : Eleanor Shriver

Grandma's Banana Nut Bread (Revised)

Preheat oven to 325 degrees; spray a 9×5 loaf pan lightly with vegetable spray.

In a large mixing bowl cream margarine and sugar, add eggs and mashed banana. Combine flour, soda and salt; gradually add to the creamed mixture stirring only until well mixed. Pour batter into prepared loaf pan. Bake in 325 degree oven for about 45 minutes or until wooden pick comes out clean.

vegetable spray
½ cup margarine
1 cup sugar
1 egg + 1 egg white
3 bananas, mashed
1½ cups all-purpose flour
½ cup whole wheat flour
1 teaspoon soda
dash salt
⅓ cup chopped nuts (optional)

Yield: 16 slices

Freezes well.
Can be baked in 2 medium 8×4 loaf pans or 4 mini loaf pans.

Cal	Prot	Fat	Carb	Fiber	Chol	Sodium
180kc	3g	6g	29g	1g	10mg	160mg

Nut Bread

3 cups flour
4 tsp. baking powder
1 tsp. salt
1 cup sugar
1 egg
1 cup milk
1 tblsp. Spry or margarine
¾ cup chopped nuts

Combine flour, baking powder, salt and sugar. Beat egg until light add milk & mix. Add dry ingredients and nuts to egg mixture. Mix lightly until ingredients are combined. Batter should not be smooth appearing. Pour into a greased loaf pan. Bake 350 degrees, one hour.

Cal	Prot	Fat	Carb	Fiber	Chol	Sodium
190kc	4g	5g	32g	1g	15mg	290mg

Nut Bread (Revised)

Preheat oven to 350 degrees; spray a 5×9 loaf pan with vegetable spray.

Combine flour, baking powder, salt and sugar. Beat egg slightly, add milk and margarine, beating until blended. Add dry ingredients and nuts to milk mixture, stir lightly just until all ingredients are blended. Batter will not be smooth appearing. Pour into prepared pan. Bake 350 degrees, one hour.

Yield: 16 slices

vegetable spray
3 cups all-purpose flour*
4 teaspoons baking powder
½ teaspoon salt
1 cup sugar
1 egg
1 cup reduced-fat milk
1 tablespoon margarine, melted
½ cup chopped nuts

*Can substitute 1 cup whole wheat flour.

Cal	Prot	Fat	Carb	Fiber	Chol	Sodium
180kc	4g	4g	32g	<1g	10mg	220mg

Breads & Breakfast

Nanny's French Toast

1 loaf French bread
8–9 eggs
2 cups milk
3 tablespoons brown sugar
1 tablespoon butter
cinnamon

Slice enough bread to cover bottom of large baking pan. Mix eggs, milk, sugar and butter, pour over bread, sprinkle with cinnamon. Leave it set for an hour or so in the refrigerator.

Cook piece by piece in a hot greased iron skillet or bake the whole pan in medium oven until liquids set.

Cal	Prot	Fat	Carb	Fiber	Chol	Sodium
130kc	6g	4.5g	17g	<1g	100mg	200mg

Baked Raisin French Toast (Revised)

Spray a 9×13 baking pan with vegetable spray. Evenly spread cream cheese over 8 slices of bread, place bread in prepared pan; top with remaining slices of bread. In a medium mixing bowl whisk egg and egg substitute until well blended. Add milk and syrup, stir well. Pour over bread; cover and refrigerate overnight. About 1½ hours before serving, remove pan from refrigerator, let stand about 30 minutes. Meanwhile, preheat oven to 350 degrees. Bake at 350 degrees for 45–50 minutes or until baked through.

Yield: 8 servings

vegetable spray
16 slices raisin bread
one 8 ounce package fat-
    free cream cheese
2 whole eggs
2 egg whites
1 cup egg substitute
2 cups skim milk
½ cup maple syrup
cinnamon
nutmeg

Cal	Prot	Fat	Carb	Fiber	Chol	Sodium
130kc	6g	3.5g	17g	2g	17mg	200mg

Breads and Breakfast

These dumplings are good as a side dish with chicken, you can simply use fat-free canned chicken broth. I also substitute dumplings instead of noodles in my chicken soup occasionally.

Isabelle's Fluffy Dumplings

stew or broth
1 egg
¾ cup milk
2 cups all-purpose flour
3 teaspoons baking powder
½ teaspoon salt
1 tablespoon melted butter or margarine

Have stew simmering. Beat egg in a mixing bowl, add milk and butter, sift in dry ingredients; beat well. Dip teaspoon into hot stew, then into dough, drop by the teaspoonfuls into simmering stew. Cover and cook 10–12 minutes, uncover and cook until wooden pick comes out clean.

Yield: approximately 36 dumplings

Recipe from: Isabelle Shriver Smail

Cal	Prot	Fat	Carb	Fiber	Chol	Sodium
35kc	1g	.5g	6g	0g	5mg	80mg

Cooking with Grandma and the Girls

Growing up in the south, my family wouldn't consider a holiday meal complete without corn bread dressing to compliment the poultry. Mom never used a recipe but simply made her dressing by a handful of this and a pinch of that. The day before making the dressing she would bake a recipe of corn bread in an iron skillet, which she would cool and store until she was ready to make the dressing. Over the years I have never been able to duplicate her dressing, but several years ago I found this recipe and thought it was very similar to hers. I used it until we got serious about fat consumption then I revised it slightly. In the revised version you will see little change in taste or texture but a significant change in fat content.

Southern Corn Bread Dressing

one 9″ skillet corn bread

10 slices stale white bread

1 tablespoon ground sage

½ teaspoon oregano

¼ teaspoon pepper

½ teaspoon ground thyme

⅛ teaspoon garlic powder

dash paprika

dash tarragon

dash lemon pepper

¼ cup butter

½ cup chopped celery

½ cup chopped onion

4 cups turkey giblet broth

2 eggs, beaten

Crumble corn bread and white bread in a large bowl; add seasonings, set aside. Melt butter, add celery and onions, sauté until browned. Add to bread and seasonings in bowl; add eggs and broth. Stir just until moistened, add more broth if you as needed to make moist. Spoon 9 × 13 baking pan and bake at 350 degrees for about 1 hour.

Cal	Prot	Fat	Carb	Fiber	Chol	Sodium
171kc	7g	7g	20g	1g	44mg	700mg

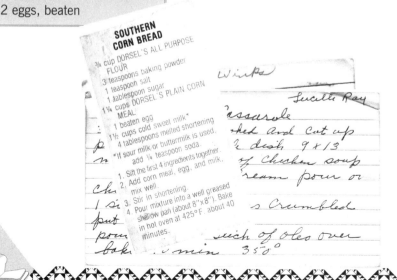

Southern Corn Bread Dressing (Revised)

vegetable spray
1 recipe Corn Bread,* page 12
5–6 stale biscuits,** page 9 or
   stale bread
1 tablespoon ground sage
1 teaspoon poultry seasoning
¼ teaspoon pepper
1 tablespoon margarine
1 cup chopped celery
1 cup chopped onion
4 cups turkey giblet broth***
   or chicken fat-free,
   low-sodium broth
1 egg + 1 egg white, beaten

Preheat oven to 350 degrees; spray two 9″ iron skillets or one 9×13 baking dish with vegetable spray. Crumble corn bread and 5–6 biscuits in a large bowl; add sage, poultry seasoning, and pepper, set aside. Melt butter in a medium skillet, add celery and onions, sauté until browned. Add onions to bread and seasonings in bowl; add egg whites and broth. Stir just until moistened. (The amount of broth used depends on how moist or firm you want the dressing.) Spoon into prepared baking dish, bake in 350 degree oven for about 1 hour.

*Add 1 cup frozen corn kernels, thawed and drained, for a nice variation.
**I serve biscuits 1–2 days before Christmas and make enough to have leftovers.
***If you are not using giblet broth; skim off all visible fat from plain broth and shred about
   ½–1 cup cooked chicken or turkey for added texture.

Cal	Prot	Fat	Carb	Fiber	Chol	Sodium
159kc	7g	4g	23g	1g	23mg	756mg

Cornmeal Mush

My mom always served a hot breakfast for her family. In the winter, she would often make oatmeal, cream of wheat or cornmeal mush, served with sugar and milk. As a young adult I started hearing about Polenta, which is a cornmeal based dish. Little did I know, this was basically the same thing as my mom's cornmeal mush! It is simply served a little differently and with different accompaniments.

Mom didn't have a specific recipe, but this is basically the same way she prepared it.

1 cup cornmeal
½ cup cold water
1 teaspoon salt
4 cups boiling water

Have water boiling in the bottom of a double boiler. Place 4 cups boiling water in top of double boiler. Combine cornmeal, salt, and cold water; gradually stir cornmeal mixture into boiling water in top of double boiler. Continue to stir 2–3 minutes. Reduce heat to low, cover pan and cook for about 20 minutes, stirring frequently. Mixture will become quite thick.

Serve hot with sugar, maple syrup, or honey, and milk.

Cal	Prot	Fat	Carb	Fiber	Chol	Sodium
100kc	3g	1g	23g	2g	0mg	375mg

Polenta

This recipe came to me through my daughter-in-law, Angie, who comes from an Italian background with many relatives in Arizona. Angie's paternal grandmother, Mary Ciochetti, known to her family as "Nanny," served polenta frequently. After cooking the cornmeal mixture, Mary would pour the polenta in a shallow round pan to set. When ready to serve; she would invert the pan onto a flat surface and cut the polenta into sections using a stout string. The following recipe is not Mary's original recipe, because she didn't use a recipe. However, she did give her family the love of this simple, tasty dish, which they continue to enjoy. In keeping with the times which we now live in, this simpler recipe for polenta was developed. Even though this is not an old recipe, the precious memories the Ciochetti family associate with polenta is very special indeed.

Maddalen Lewis, a relative of Angie's, shared the following memories:

What happy memories I have of winter Sunday evenings and holidays. The three Giacoma brothers and their families, would all get together for polenta. The men would take turns stirring the polenta. After a big dinner, we would all gather around the piano and sing Italian songs that the men had taught us.

2 quarts water
2 teaspoons salt
2 cups cornmeal
2 tablespoons butter

Combine all ingredients in an casserole. Bake in 350 degree oven for 1 hour. Stir, continue to bake 10–15 minutes more or until very thick. At this point you can either serve it warm as it is; or you can pour it into a greased shallow pan or a loaf pan, cover and chill several hours until firm. Invert polenta on flat surface; cut into serving portions and fry in a small amount of hot fat until brown. Serve with Italian sauce, grated Parmesan cheese, maple syrup, honey or your choice of accompaniments.

Yield: 10 servings

Recipe from: Maddalen Lewis

Cal	Prot	Fat	Carb	Fiber	Chol	Sodium
100kc	2g	3g	17g	2g	5mg	800mg

Grandma's Recipe for Contentment

Keep your heart free from hate, your mind free from worry. Live simply, expect little, give much, sing often, and pray always. Fill your life with love, scatter sunshine, forget self, and think of others. Do as you would be done by. These are the tried links in contentment's golden chain.

Author unknown

Soups

Chicken Noodle Soup

1 whole chicken, cut up
2 carrots
2 ribs celery
1 large onion
1 clove garlic, minced
1 bay leaf
½–1 teaspoon thyme
1 tablespoon parsley
2 teaspoons salt
½ teaspoon black pepper
egg noodles

Cook chicken pieces in soup kettle with carrot, onion, celery, and water. When chicken is tender, remove chicken; bone, cut into chunks and return to soup. Cook until everything is tender; add noodles, cook until tender.

Cal	Prot	Fat	Carb	Fiber	Chol	Sodium
340kc	22g	15g	28g	3g	95mg	580mg

Chicken Noodle Soup (Revised)

Cook chicken breast in large soup kettle with 1 peeled carrot, 1 stalk of celery, ¼ onion, garlic, bay leaf and 2 quarts of water. Cook 1 to 1½ hours or until very tender. Discard vegetables, set chicken aside to cool, cut into chunks. Chop remaining carrots, celery and onion into bite size pieces. Place all remaining ingredients, except chicken and noodles, into kettle with broth; simmer 1 hour. Add chicken and noodles,* cook for about 15 minutes.

Yield: 10 servings

*May substitute dumplings in place of noodles.

4 boneless, skinless, chicken
    breast halves
3 large carrots
3 stalks celery
1 large onion
1 large clove garlic, minced
1 bay leaf
2 quarts water
½ teaspoon thyme
1 tablespoon parsley
1 teaspoon salt
¼ teaspoon black pepper
¼ teaspoon lemon pepper
1½ quarts chicken broth
1 large Knorr chicken bouillon
    cube.
noodles as desired

Cal	Prot	Fat	Carb	Fiber	Chol	Sodium
300kc	34g	4g	32g	4g	85mg	1010mg

Soups

Broccoly (sic) Cheese Soup

3 large potatoes, finely diced

2 stalks celery

1½ tsp. parsley flakes

¾ tsp. salt

pepper to taste

1 large bunch brocolly (sic)

5 tbsp. flour

2 cups milk

¾–1 lb. Velveeta cheese, cut into cubes

Cook vegetables and seasonings in water and chicken broth to equal 3 cups liquid.

Chop brocolly (sic) into small pieces and cook till tender.

Heat milk and flour mixture, stir til smooth; add cheese cubes and heat until melted. Add brocolly (sic) to other vegetables and slowly add cheese mixture, heat carefully as cheese scorches easily.

Recipe from: Markeeta Bundscuk

Cal	Prot	Fat	Carb	Fiber	Chol	Sodium
179kc	11g	8.3g	15.7g	3g	26mg	511mg

Broccoli Cheese Soup (Revised)

Rinse, drain and coarsely chop broccoli in a food processor. Place in a medium soup kettle, along with potatoes, celery, chicken broth, parsley, salt, and pepper. Bring to a boil, reduce heat to low and simmer about 30–40 minutes or until very tender. In a quart jar combine milk and flour; shake vigorously until well blended. When vegetables are very tender, slowly add flour mixture, stirring constantly until it starts to thicken. Add cheese cubes and continue to stir until melted, watch carefully as cheese scorches easily; do not let it come to a boil.

Yield: 12 cups

1 large bunch broccoli

3 large potatoes, diced

2 stalks celery, diced

3 cups chicken broth

2 teaspoons dried parsley flakes

½ teaspoon salt

freshly ground black pepper to taste

5 tablespoons all-purpose flour

2 cups reduced-fat milk

½ lb. reduced-fat processed cheese, (cut into cubes)*

*Can substitute shredded fat-free or reduced-fat sharp Cheddar cheese.

Cal	Prot	Fat	Carb	Fiber	Chol	Sodium
140kc	12g	3g	19g	3g	13mg	541mg

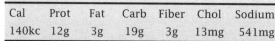

Golden Cheese Soup

3 cups chopped potatoes
1 cup water
½ cup celery slices
½ cup carrot slices
¼ cup chopped onion
1 tsp parsley flakes
1 chicken bouillon cube
½ tsp salt
dash pepper
1½ cups milk
2 tblsp flour
½ lb Velveeta cheese, cubed

In a large saucepan, combine the first nine ingredients. Cover, simmer 15–20 minutes or until vegetables are tender. Gradually add milk to flour, mixing until well blended. Add milk mixture to vegetables; cook until thickened. Add Velveeta cheese; stir until melted.

Yield: 6–8 servings

I like to double the recipe using 3 cups of potatoes, 1½ cups broccoli and 1½ cups cauliflower.

Cal	Prot	Fat	Carb	Fiber	Chol	Sodium
214kc	13g	10g	20g	2g	36mg	1000mg

Recipe from: Caroline Shriver

Golden Cheese Soup (Revised)

In a large saucepan, combine the first nine ingredients. Bring mixture to a boil; reduce heat and simmer 30–40 minutes or until vegetables are very tender. Using a quart jar combine milk and flour, shake until well blended. Pour into a small saucepan, cook over medium heat until mixture starts to bubble and thicken, add cheese, stir constantly until cheese is melted, being careful not to let cheese scorch. Add milk mixture to vegetables; cook until thickened.

Yield: six 1-cup servings

*Substitute 1½ cup reduced-fat milk and ½ cup fat-free half-and-half.
**Velveeta, Healthy Choice, etc.

3 cups chopped potatoes
2 cups water
½ cup sliced celery
½ cup grated carrot
¼ cup chopped onion
1 teaspoon parsley flakes
1 chicken bouillon cube or 1
    teaspoon chicken base
½ teaspoon salt
freshly ground black pepper to
    taste
2 cups reduced-fat milk*
¼ cup all-purpose flour
8 ounces reduced-fat
    processed cheese, cubed**
Tabasco sauce (optional)

Cal	Prot	Fat	Carb	Fiber	Chol	Sodium
190kc	14g	6g	25g	2g	26mg	975mg

Soups

Midwest Clam Chowder

2 cups diced potatoes
½ cup sliced carrots
½ cup celery
⅛ cup onion
1½ tsp. salt
¼ tsp. pepper
2 cups boiling water
¼ cup margarine
¼ cup flour
2 cups milk
10 oz. Cheddar cheese
2 cups cream style corn
1 small can minced clams

Combine potatoes, carrots, celery, onion, salt & pepper. Add water, simmer 10 minutes, do not drain. Make a cheese sauce with margarine, flour & milk; add cheese, stirring till melted. Add corn & clams to vegetable mixture, slowly add cheese sauce and heat soup mixture. Do not boil.

Yield: 6–8 servings

Cal	Prot	Fat	Carb	Fiber	Chol	Sodium
330kc	14g	19g	28g	2g	45mg	1020mg

Midwest Clam Chowder (Revised)

Using a medium soup kettle; combine potatoes, carrots, celery, onion, water, salt, and pepper. Bring to a boil, reduce heat and simmer about 30–40 minutes, or until very tender. Heat milk slightly to take chill off then combine with flour in a quart jar, shake until well blended, add to vegetable mixture, stirring constantly until mixture starts to bubble and thicken. Add cheese, stir constantly until melted,being careful not to let cheese scorch; add corn and clams. Continue to simmer, stirring constantly until thoroughly hot. Be careful to not let mixture boil.

Yield: 9 (1-cup) servings

*If fat-free half-and-half is not available use 2 cups reduced-fat milk.
**Substitute 8 oz. reduced-fat processed cheese, i.e. Velveeta, Healthy Choice, etc.

2 cups diced potatoes
½ cup sliced carrots
½ cup sliced celery
½ cup chopped onion
2 cups water
½ teaspoon salt
freshly ground black pepper to taste
¼ cup all-purpose flour
1½ cups reduced-fat milk
½ cup fat-free half-and-half*
8 oz reduced-fat sharp Cheddar cheese*
2 cups cream style corn
1 (6 ½ oz.) can minced clams

Cal	Prot	Fat	Carb	Fiber	Chol	Sodium
170kc	12g	2.5g	27g	3g	10mg	650mg

Soups

Oyster Stew

Oyster Stew was a favorite of my mom and John's dad. They both looked forward to the months with an "r" in it, since this was the only time fresh oysters were available.

> 2 cups milk
> 1 pint oysters
> butter to season
> salt & pepper to taste

In a small sauce pan heat milk until just scalded, add oysters & liquid continue to cook just until everything is hot and oysters are plump and edges start to curl. Add butter, salt, and pepper. Serve immediately with oyster crackers.

Cal	Prot	Fat	Carb	Fiber	Chol	Sodium
239kc	7g	16g	7g	0g	64mg	773mg

Oyster Stew (Revised)

Heat water in bottom of double boiler to boiling. Melt margarine in top of a double boiler, add onion and celery and sauté until tender. Add milk, half and half, and oysters with liquids to onion mixture, place over the boiling water in bottom pan.

Heat just until everything is hot and the oysters are plump and start to float to top. Add salt, black and cayenne peppers. Serve immediately, garnish with chopped chives.

Yield: 4 small servings

> 1 tablespoon margarine
> 2 tablespoons minced onion
> 1 tablespoon minced celery
> 1½ cups reduced fat milk
> ½ cup fat-free half and half
> 1 pint oysters
> ½ teaspoon salt
> freshly ground black pepper
>   to taste
> dash cayenne pepper
> chopped chives

Cal	Prot	Fat	Carb	Fiber	Chol	Sodium
124kc	91g	6g	10g	0g	30mg	693mg

Cooking with Grandma and the Girls

Soups

In the Shriver family, when a young man turned twelve years of age, he was permitted to go deer hunting with the men of the family. This became an annual ritual for my husband John, his dad, and his brother Tom. Our son, Johnny, had the opportunity to go a few times as well. They hunted many, many years, until John's father's health no longer permitted him to go. John and his brother Tom would travel home from wherever they lived at the time to go deer hunting. Since buck season started the Monday after Thanksgiving, when our children were younger, we would go as a family for Thanksgiving, staying the week with John's mom while the men hunted. The men would leave on Sunday after Thanksgiving for hunting camp while the women and children stayed home doing lots of fun things through the week. However, the Saturday before the men left, all the women were busy in the kitchen preparing food to go along to camp with them. John's mom would boil potatoes, which the men would slice and fry with a sausage they bought up there, and she always made a huge kettle of her special vegetable beef soup, plus lots of homemade cookies.

Soups

Mom's Vegetable-Beef Soup

Tom told me the secret to his mom's delicious soup was the rump roast.

rump roast, short ribs of beef,
   or chuck,
soup bone
mixed vegetables
potatoes, celery, and cabbage
1 can tomato soup
parsley flakes, salt & pepper

Cook beef and soup bone until tender, remove bone and discard. Add vegetables, tomato soup and seasonings; cook for several hours on low heat until vegetables are nice and tender.

Recipe from: Eleanor Shriver

Mom's Vegetable Soup (Revised)

Cook soup bone in enough water to cover in a large kettle; simmer for about 2 hours. Add the beef chunks, cook on low heat about 1 hour or until tender; remove bone, discard. (Unless you want the marrow.) Add remaining ingredients; continue to cook on low heat for several hours until vegetables are tender.

This gets better each day you reheat it!

Yield: 8 servings

1 soup bone
2 pounds rump of beef, cut into chunks
1 medium onion, cut into wedges
1 (16 oz.) bag of frozen mixed vegetables
3 potatoes, diced
2 stalks celery, sliced
¼ head cabbage, sliced
1 (10 oz.) can low-fat, low-sodium
   condensed tomato soup
1 bay leaf
1 teaspoon salt and black pepper to taste

Cal	Prot	Fat	Carb	Fiber	Chol	Sodium
290kc	23g	11g	26g	5g	65mg	380mg

Mr. Brunner's Cough Syrup*

Mr. Brunner loved warm comforting soups. But when he was ailing, he resorted to the following cough syrup. Mom and Dad Shriver thought it worked really well. This is especially surprising in view of the fact that neither of them would drink alcoholic beverages.

Put 1 oz. glycerin into a ½ pint bottle, add 1 box rock candy; shake and let dissolve, fill bottle up with whiskey.

*I do not recommend using this recipe since I am neither a physician nor a pharmacist. I have included it simply for the folklore. If you need further dietary aid for a lingering cough try some of Mom's chicken soup (page 29).

Salads
and
Salad Dressings

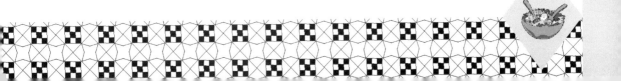

Salads

Mom Shriver was truly a natural born hostess, she loved entertaining, whether it was overnight or just having friends over for a meal. One of my first impressions of her was her cheerful disposition and her ability to run such a smooth household. Mom kept a very clean house and one of the few situations in which I saw her frustrated was when they would receive a load of coal for the old coal furnace. After the dust settled, Mom would attack the house like a whirlwind, cleaning everything, including washing walls and curtains because the coal dust would settle everywhere. Once the house was clean again, she was back to her easy-going ways.

Mom especially looked forward to hostessing a group of ladies who referred to themselves as "the girls" or "the gang." They met monthly to work on sewing projects, and remained a group for thirty-five or forty years. If she wasn't entertaining "the gang," it might be a group from church or it could even be a group of neighbors and friends for a baby shower. No matter who it was, she always put her best effort into presenting delicious food and a warm welcome. During these social gatherings, she would often serve one of her special "luncheons." The menu would consist of a Jell-O salad or maybe chicken salad, with hot rolls, beverage and always one of her wonderful desserts or plates full of freshly baked cookies. Everyone looked forward to a gathering at Eleanor Shriver's; not only did they have warm fellowship with each other, and ate sumptuous foods, but she often sent them home with "just a little something for the family." This "little something" could be a plate of cookies or a whole pie, she was so gracious and generous in sharing what she had.

SALADS

Apple Salad

8 apples, peeled & diced
2 cups cabbage, finely chopped
cover with boiled dressing made
   from the following ingredients:
2 egg yolks
1 gill vinegar
2 gills milk
1 tablespoon butter
1 tsp salt
1 tsp mustard
¼ tsp. pepper
1 tablespoon sugar

Carefully mix and cook in double boiler. The cabbage should be soaked in cold water 1 hour before chopping and the dressing should be cold. Mix cabbage, apples and salad dressing just before serving, add 2 cups finely chopped roasted peanuts

Cal	Prot	Fat	Carb	Fiber	Chol	Sodium
195kc	52g	12g	24g	9g	59mg	366mg

Apple-Cabbage Salad (Revised)

Blend flour with sugar in a small saucepan; add water and egg, blending well with flour mixture. Add mustard and vinegar; stirring constantly, cook over medium-low heat until thick and clear. Stir in salt and margarine, set aside to cool.

While dressing is cooling: Soak cabbage in ice water for 20–30 minutes; drain very well. Lift into a large bowl add apples; pour dressing over all and toss gently to coat. Spoon into serving dish; sprinkle nuts over all.

Yield: 10 servings

*Use crisp juicy apples, i.e., Jonathan, Wine sap, Macintosh, etc.

1 tablespoon all-purpose flour
½ cup sugar
1 cup water
1 egg
1 teaspoon yellow mustard
¼ cup white vinegar
dash of salt
1 teaspoon margarine
2 cups sweet, crisp apples, diced*
2 cups shredded cabbage
½ cup thinly sliced celery
¼ cup chopped nuts

Cal	Prot	Fat	Carb	Fiber	Chol	Sodium
90kc	2g	3g	16g	1g	20mg	40mg

Salads

Broccoli Salad

1 bunch broccoli, chopped
½ bunch green onions
½ cup diced celery
½ lb. bacon fried crisp & cut
2 handful raisins, golden &
    brown
Dressing:
1 tsp. vinegar
⅓ cup sugar
1 cup mayonnaise

Mix and refrigerate to chill.

Cal	Prot	Fat	Carb	Fiber	Chol	Sodium
280kc	8g	21g	19g	3g	25mg	370mg

Recipe from: Maggie Hunter

Broccoli Salad (Revised)

In a large mixing bowl combine broccoli, onions, celery and raisins. In a small bowl combine vinegar, sugar and mayonnaise, pour over salad, toss gently. Cover and refrigerate for several hours. When ready to serve, toss gently and sprinkle crumbled bacon over top.

Yield: 14 servings

*Can substitute dried cranberries or cherries.
**These are available in most groceries in bottles, if not available use 2 slices reduced-fat bacon, broiled and crumbled.

1 head broccoli, chopped
6 green onions, sliced
½ cup finely diced celery
1 cup raisins, golden or brown*
1½ teaspoon white wine vinegar
2 tablespoons sugar
1 cup reduced-fat mayonnaise
1 tablespoon real bacon pieces**

Cal	Prot	Fat	Carb	Fiber	Chol	Sodium
120kc	3g	6g	17g	3g	5mg	170mg

Cooking with Grandma and the Girls

This is a really great salad for Thanksgiving or Christmas, or when you just want something different. You can buy fresh cranberries and freeze, or you can usually find them year round in your grocer's freezer.

Fresh Cranberry Salad

1 lb. bag fresh cranberries

2 cups sugar

3 medium oranges

1 tablespoon plain gelatin

¼ cup cold water

1 (3 oz.) pkg. lemon Jell-O

1¾ cups boiling water

1¾ cup cold water

½ cup chopped celery

½ cup chopped walnuts or pecans*

Coarsely chop cranberries in food processor or grinder. Grate rind from oranges and squeeze juice. In a saucepan combine cranberries, sugar, orange juice and rind. Bring mixture to a boil; reduce heat and cook about 10 minutes; cool.

Dissolve plain gelatin in ¼ cup cold water. Dissolve lemon Jell-O in boiling water, add dissolved gelatin, stir well; add remaining 1¾ cups cold water, stir. Refrigerate until mixture begins to thicken, about the consistency of egg whites. Add cranberry mixture, celery and nuts. Pour into 9×13 or 10×10" dish; refrigerate several hours until firm.

Yield: 12 servings

*To reduce fat grams and calories use ¼ cup or less chopped nuts.

Cal	Prot	Fat	Carb	Fiber	Chol	Sodium
230kc	2g	3.5g	49g	3g	0mg	35mg

Here's what's cookin' Frozen Delight Sal. Serves 9
Recipe from the kitchen of Mae Held.
1 - 8 oz pkg cream cheese
¼ cup maple syrup
1 " whipped topping mix
½ " chopped dates
½ " maraschino cherries
½ " " nuts
1½ cup diced Pineapple (drained)
Stir cream cheese till soft & fluffy, add syrup, fruit + nuts. Fold in whipped cream. Freeze in an 8 in pan.

T his is the way my mom made her coleslaw. I always thought it was so good.

Coleslaw

½ head cabbage, shredded
1 carrot, shredded
vinegar
a sprinkle of sugar
milk, enough to moisten
couple heaping tablespoons
    mayonnaise
salt & pepper

Recipe from: Oma Day

Mix everything together.

Cal	Prot	Fat	Carb	Fiber	Chol	Sodium
130kc	1g	11g	5g	2g	10mg	95mg

Coleslaw (Revised)

Place cabbage and carrot in large bowl; combine remaining ingredients; pour over cabbage mixture and stir. Add salt and pepper as desired.

Yield: 8 servings

4 cups shredded cabbage
1 carrot, shredded
¾ teaspoon vinegar
1 tablespoon sugar
3 tablespoon reduced-fat milk
½ cup reduced-fat mayonnaise
salt and pepper, to taste

Cal	Prot	Fat	Carb	Fiber	Chol	Sodium
59kc	1g	3g	6g	1g	5mg	33mg

Cucumber Garden Salad

Cucumber garden salad is a popular German dish, common in areas where there was a heavy population of German settlers.

3 cucumbers, sliced thin
1 onion, chopped
2 tablespoons parsley
salt and pepper
½ cup sugar
¼ cup dark vinegar
¾ cup sour cream*

Mix cucumbers, onion, and parsley; sprinkle with salt and pepper. Stir sugar into the vinegar and sour cream; spoon over cucumbers and onions. Serve with beef or pork.

Yield: 6 servings

* To reduce fat grams and calories; substitute reduced fat or fat-free sour cream and reduce sugar to ⅓ cup.

Original nutrition data:

Cal	Prot	Fat	Carb	Fiber	Chol	Sodium
122kc	2g	4g	23g	1g	7mg	44mg

Reduced fat nutrition data:

Cal	Prot	Fat	Carb	Fiber	Chol	Sodium
112kc	3g	0g	26g	2g	3.5mg	86mg

Creamy Cucumbers

Layer cucumbers and onion in a bowl; mix remaining ingredients, pour over sliced vegetables. Cover and store in refrigerator until ready to use.

Yield: 8 servings

*To reduce fat grams and calories, substitute reduced fat mayonnaise and reduce sugar to ⅓ cup.

4 medium cucumbers, peeled and sliced
1 small sweet onion, sliced thin
1 cup mayonnaise
4 tablespoons white vinegar
½ cup sugar
¼ teaspoon salt

Original nutrition data:

Cal	Prot	Fat	Carb	Fiber	Chol	Sodium
184kc	1g	10g	25g	<1g	8mg	230mg

Reduced fat nutrition data:

Cal	Prot	Fat	Carb	Fiber	Chol	Sodium
100kc	1.2g	3.3g	18g	<1g	5mg	335mg

Salads

Wilted Lettuce

My mom used to make this with freshly picked lettuce straight from Dad's garden.

3 tblsp. bacon grease
½ cup water
¼ cup vinegar
1 tsp sugar
mess of leaf lettuce
2 green onions, sliced

Bring bacon grease, water, vinegar and sugar to a boil, pour over clean, dry lettuce and onions, toss gently. Serve immediately.

Cal	Prot	Fat	Carb	Fiber	Chol	Sodium
120kc	1g	10g	7g	2g	5mg	75mg

Wilted Lettuce (Revised)

Combine oil, water, vinegar and sugar in a sauce pan, bring to a boil, pour over clean, dry lettuce and onions, toss gently. Sprinkle with bacon pieces. Serve immediately.

Yield: 4 servings

*These are available in most groceries in bottles, if not available use 2 slices reduced-fat bacon, broiled and crumbled.

2 tablespoons vegetable oil
½ cup water
¼ cup vinegar
1 teaspoon sugar
1 medium bunch very fresh leaf lettuce
3 green onions, sliced
1 tablespoon real bacon pieces*

Cal	Prot	Fat	Carb	Fiber	Chol	Sodium
121kc	2g	8g	17g	2g	1mg	70mg

Cooking with Grandma and the Girls

Salads

I remember nice summer days when Dad Shriver would take the family to Kittanning for a boat ride on the Allegheny River. After cruising the river (with a possible trip through the locks), we would find a nice spot at the riverside park to dock the boat. There, in the shade of old, magnificent trees and grass as soft as down, we would relax, go for a swim or join in a game of badminton. Eventually, a fire was started and, after it burned down to red hot coals, we would cook hamburgers and hotdogs. Mom Shriver always had baskets and coolers packed with goodies for our picnic, which always included either her famous potato salad or equally famous macaroni salad. Added to that were baked beans, sliced tomatoes, onion, and pickles. In case you were still looking for something else, there would be fresh fruit, maybe a watermelon or homegrown peaches, depending on what Genito's fruit stand featured the day before. Of course, no meal was complete without something from Mom's oven—it might be a chocolate cake with white icing or some freshly baked cookies, usually Toll House chocolate chip. After partaking of the feast, we would drift off to a shady spot under one of the wonderful, old trees to stretch out and maybe take a short nap before heading back to the river where we would continue to ride, ski, and swim until the sun started to set. As the sun was setting, we would load the car with empty coolers and baskets then head towards home, contentedly, deliciously exhausted from the long day of play. Those were truly the good old summer days.

Mom's Potato Salad

8–10 medium potatoes, boiled
    with skin on
4 hard-cooked eggs,** diced
⅓ cup chopped celery
⅓ cup chopped onion
½ cup chopped sweet or dill
    pickles*
1 (4 oz.) jar chopped pimento
salt & pepper to taste
3 tablespoon sugar
1 teaspoon cider vinegar
2 teaspoon yellow mustard

Peel and dice potatoes while warm; put in a large bowl, add eggs, celery, onion, pickles, pimento, salt, and pepper. In a small bowl combine sugar, vinegar, mustard and mayonnaise, pour over vegetables, toss gently to coat. Dressing coats best if potatoes are still warm. Sprinkle with paprika, refrigerate.

Original nutrition data:

Cal	Prot	Fat	Carb	Fiber	Chol	Sodium
181kc	4g	9g	23g	4g	96mg	185mg

Yield: 12 servings

*Sometimes Mom would use cucumber instead of pickles and use more vinegar.
**To reduce fat grams and calories, I simply discard 2 egg yolks and use reduced-fat or fat-free mayonnaise.

Reduced fat nutrition data:

Cal	Prot	Fat	Carb	Fiber	Chol	Sodium
118kc	8g	3g	19g	4g	49mg	218mg

Salads

Mom's Potato Salad For A Reunion

10 lb. potatoes, cooked & diced
1 dozen hard boiled eggs, chopped
1 cup chopped sweet pickles
2 cups finely chopped celery
2 (4 oz.) jars chopped pimento
1 medium onion, chopped
1–2 teaspoon salt or to taste
½ teaspoon black pepper or to taste
½ cup + 1 tablespoon sugar
1 tablespoon vinegar
3 tablespoons yellow mustard
3 cups mayonnaise

Follow preceding directions. Again using reduced fat or fat-free mayonnaise and eliminating some of the egg yolks for less fat calories and cholesterol.

Yield: 32 servings

Cal	Prot	Fat	Carb	Fiber	Chol	Sodium
181kc	4g	9g	23g	4g	96mg	185mg

Macaroni Salad

Follow basic recipe for Mom's potato salad on page 46 except substitute 2 cups uncooked macaroni for potatoes, cooked according to directions and drained. Substitute dill pickles for sweet pickles.

Yield: 12 servings

Cal	Prot	Fat	Carb	Fiber	Chol	Sodium
149kc	3g	9g	15g	<1g	96mg	180mg

Kartoffel Salad—Hot German Potato Salad

2 lb. potatoes
6 slices bacon, crisply cooked,
    crumbled
⅓ cup bacon drippings
¼ cup vinegar
salt
1 tablespoon sugar
1 medium onion, diced

Boil potatoes in their jackets until done; peel and slice. Heat bacon drippings, vinegar, salt, and sugar. Combine hot potato slices, crumbled bacon and onion in large bowl. Pour over this, the dressing and toss lightly, being careful not to break potatoes.

Cal	Prot	Fat	Carb	Fiber	Chol	Sodium
250kc	4g	12g	32g	3g	15mg	135mg

Kartoffel Salad
Hot German Potato Salad (Revised)

Boil potatoes in their jackets until tender; peel and slice thin, cover and set aside in a warm place. Pour olive oil into a large skillet. Add onions to hot oil and sauté until golden brown. Stirring constantly, add flour, salt, sugar, and celery seeds, cook until smooth and bubbly. Gradually add water and vinegar, continuing to stir; bring to a boil, boil 1 minute. Place warm potato slices in a large bowl, pour the dressing over all and toss lightly, being careful not to break potatoes. Sprinkle pepper and bacon pieces over all. Serve warm.

2 lb. potatoes, (6–7 medium)
2 tablespoons olive oil
¾ cup chopped onion
2 tablespoons all-purpose flour
½ teaspoon salt
1½ tablespoons sugar
½ teaspoon celery seeds
¾ cup water
⅓ cup vinegar
freshly ground black pepper
2 tablespoons real bacon pieces*

Yield: 8 servings

*These are available on your grocers shelf, be careful to get "real" and not "imitation."

Cal	Prot	Fat	Carb	Fiber	Chol	Sodium
190kc	4g	4.5g	35g	3g	0mg	180mg

Salads

Salads

Macaroni Dandy Salad

3 oz. elbow macaroni cook & drain
½ cup mayonnaise
1 tablespoon lemon juice
1 teaspoon salt
1 teaspoon sugar
¼ teaspoon celery seed
4 eggs, boiled & chopped
1 cucumber, chopped
1 tomato, diced
1 cup diced celery
3 tablespoons chopped pimento
2 tablespoons chopped green pepper

Mix mayonnaise with lemon juice, salt & sugar. Combine with macaroni, celery seed, eggs, cucumber, tomato, celery, pimento, and green pepper. Serve on salad greens, garnish with radishes.

Yield: 6–8 servings.

Recipe from: Maggie Hunter

Cal	Prot	Fat	Carb	Fiber	Chol	Sodium
160kc	4g	13g	6g	<1g	105mg	410mg

Macaroni Dandy Salad (Revised)

Cook macaroni according to package directions; drain. Combine mayonnaise, lemon juice, sugar, salt and celery seed, set aside. Discard 2 egg yolks, chop remaining egg whites and 2 whole eggs. In a large mixing bowl combine macaroni, egg, cucumber, celery, pimento, and green pepper. Pour mayonnaise mixture over all and gently toss. Serve on salad greens, garnish with radishes or tomato wedges.

Yield: 8 servings.

2 cups elbow macaroni
½ cup reduced-fat mayonnaise
1½ tablespoons lemon juice
3 teaspoons sugar
½ teaspoon salt
½ teaspoon celery seed
4 hard boiled eggs
1 cucumber, chopped
1 cup diced celery
1 (2 oz.) jar chopped pimento
2 tablespoons chopped green pepper
lettuce, optional
radishes, optional
tomatoes, optional

Cal	Prot	Fat	Carb	Fiber	Chol	Sodium
200kc	7g	8g	25g	1g	100mg	310mg

Tomato-Cucumber Salad

2 tomatoes, peeled and diced
1 cucumber, peeled and cut up
1 small onion, diced or sliced
½ cup sugar
½ cup vegetable oil
¼ cup vinegar
1 tsp. salt
½ tsp. pepper

Mix and let stand several hours. You may use left over dressing again.

Cal	Prot	Fat	Carb	Fiber	Chol	Sodium
360kc	1g	27g	31g	1g	0mg	590mg

Tomato-Cucumber Salad (Revised)

Alternately layer tomatoes, cucumber and onion in a clear shallow bowl. Combine sugar and water in a microwave safe cup, microwave 1 minute on high; stir to dissolve. Cool slightly, add vinegar, oil and salt; pour over vegetables, sprinkle pepper over all.

Yield: 4 servings

2 medium ripe tomatoes, sliced
1 medium cucumber, sliced
½ small mild onion, sliced
⅓ cup sugar
¼ cup water
¼ cup vinegar
¼ cup vegetable oil
½ teaspoon salt
dash freshly ground black pepper

Cal	Prot	Fat	Carb	Fiber	Chol	Sodium
200kc	1g	14g	21g	<1g	0mg	300mg

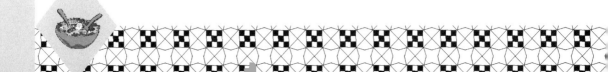

Salads

Lime Jell-O Fruit Cocktail Salad

This was Mom Shriver's favorite lime-fruit cocktail Jell-O salad.

Heat one large can or two small cans fruit cocktail, pour over one package lime Jell-O. Stir until dissolved, let stand until slightly jelled. Break one package Philadelphia cream cheese into small pieces, add to ½ cup cream and whip until stiff, then combine with gelatin mixture and beat well. Pour into shallow pan or mold and put into refrigerator for two hours or longer. Garnish with cherries.

Cal	Prot	Fat	Carb	Fiber	Chol	Sodium
360kc	5g	8g	71g	5g	25mg	100mg

Lime Jell-O Fruit Cocktail Salad (Revised)

1 (6 oz.) pkg. lime Jell-O
2 cups boiling water
cold water
1 (17 oz.) can fruit cocktail,
   reserve juice
1 (8 oz.) pkg. reduced-fat
   cream cheese
1 cup reduced-fat or fat-free
   nondairy whipped topping
¼ cup maraschino cherries,
   cut in half
reduced-fat mayonnaise

Dissolve Jell-O in boiling water, stir until clear. Drain fruit cocktail, add cold water to juice to make 1½ cups*; add to Jell-O, stir. Refrigerate until slightly thickened, about the consistency of egg whites. While Jell-O is chilling: Using a fork blend cream cheese and whipped topping until smooth. Add fruit and cream cheese mixture to Jell-O, blend thoroughly. Pour into a 9×13″ or 10×10″ dish; cover and refrigerate about one hour. Garnish top with cherry halves, return to refrigerator and chill for several hours or overnight, until very firm. To serve cut into squares and serve on individual salad plates lined with lettuce, add a small dollop of mayonnaise to each serving.

Yield: 15 servings

Recipe from: Mary Jane Walton

* Or use only 1¼ cups cold liquid to make in a mold.
From: Mary Jane Walton
**While Mom Shriver always used fruit cocktail, Ruby Wick's recipe called for canned pears, drained and mashed with a fork. This gives the salad a totally different texture.

Cal	Prot	Fat	Carb	Fiber	Chol	Sodium
140kc	3g	6g	18g	0g	10mg	105mg

Grandma Shriver's lime Jell-O-vegetable salad was our daughter, Audrey's, favorite. Audrey has fond memories of a square of the Jell-O salad placed on a leaf of lettuce, with a dollop of mayonnaise to top it off which she and her cousins liked to spread over the entire top of their Jell-O square. She now serves it to her family and friends.

Salads

Health Salad

1 (6 oz.) box lime Jell-O
2 cups boiling water
1½ cups cold water
1 cup shredded carrots
¾ cup thinly sliced celery
½ cup chopped nuts**
mayonnaise**

Dissolve Jell-O in boiling water, add cold water; refrigerate. Chill until the consistency of egg whites; stir in carrots, celery, and nuts. Pour into a 9×13" or 10×10" dish; refrigerate until firm. . To serve cut into squares and serve in individual salad plates lined with lettuce, add a small dollop of mayonnaise to each serving.

Yield: 15 servings

*There are many variations of this wonderful salad. You can use lemon Jell-O or add drained crushed pineapple or add raisins. Use your imagination.
**To reduce fat grams and calories reduce nuts to ¼ cup or use raisins instead, and substitute reduced-fat or fat-free mayonnaise for regular.

Recipe from: Ginny Mangus

Cal	Prot	Fat	Carb	Fiber	Chol	Sodium
110kc	2g	6g	12g	<1g	5mg	70mg

Salads

Perfection Salad

This is a wonderful variation of the health salad; I love the crunchiness of the cabbage, carrots, and green pepper.

1 (6 oz.) pkg. lemon Jell-O
2 cups boiling water
1½ cups cold water
1 tablespoon lemon juice
1 tablespoon white vinegar
2 tablespoons minced mild onion
¾ cup shredded cabbage
½ cup shredded carrots
2 tablespoons shredded green pepper
¼ cup finely diced celery
2 tablespoons chopped pimento
lettuce

Dissolve Jell-O in boiling water, add cold water, stir; refrigerate. Chill until the consistency of egg whites; stir in cabbage, carrots, green pepper, celery, and pimento. Pour into a 9×13″ or 10×10″ dish; refrigerate until firm. To serve cut into squares and serve in individual salad plates lined with lettuce, add a small dollop of mayonnaise to each serving.

Yield: 15 servings

*To reduce fat grams and calories substitute reduced fat or fat-free mayonnaise.

Cal	Prot	Fat	Carb	Fiber	Chol	Sodium
80kc	1g	3.5g	12g	0g	5mg	70mg

Raspberry Cream Jell-O

1 small raspberry Jell-O
1 cup boiling water
1 #2 can cherry pie filling
1 small lemon Jell-O
1 cup boiling water
1 pkg. Philadelphia cream cheese
⅓ cup mayonaize (sic)
1 cup crushed pineapple
½ cup whipping cream
1 cup miniature marshmallows
¼ cup nuts

Dissolve raspberry Jell-O in 1 cup boiling water, stir in cherry pie filling, and pour into medium pan and chill.

Dissolve lemon Jell-O in 1 cup boiling water, set aside to partially chill.

Beat together cream cheese and mayonnaise until creamy, gradually add lemon Jell-O, stir in undrained pineapple, whip cream and fold in Jell-O mixture. Add marshmallows and spread over cherry layer and top with nuts.

Recipe from: Lucille Miller

Cal	Prot	Fat	Carb	Fiber	Chol	Sodium
240kc	3g	13g	27g	0g	30mg	115mg

Raspberry-Cream Jell-O (Revised)

Dissolve raspberry Jell-O in 1 cup boiling water; add cold water. Stir in cherry pie filling, pour into 9×13″ dish; refrigerate.

Dissolve lemon Jell-O in remaining 1 cup boiling water, add undrained pineapple; refrigerate until slightly thickened, about the consistency of egg whites.

In a medium bowl blend cream cheese and mayonnaise until creamy, blend into lemon Jell-O; refrigerate until slightly thickened. Blend whipped topping into lemon Jell-O mixture; spread over cherry layer and top with nuts. Refrigerate until firm.

Yield: 15 servings

1 (3 oz) pkg. raspberry Jell-O
2 cup boiling water, divided
½ cup cold water
1 (20 oz) can cherry pie filling
1 (3 oz.) pkg. lemon Jell-O
1 (3 oz.) pkg. reduced-fat
    cream cheese
⅓ cup reduced-fat mayonnaise
1 cup crushed pineapple
    undrained
½ cup reduced-fat nondairy
    whipped topping
2 tablespoons chopped nuts, if
    desired

Cal	Prot	Fat	Carb	Fiber	Chol	Sodium
150kc	2g	4.5g	25g	0g	10mg	100mg

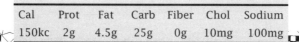

Salads

Strawberry-Sour Cream Jell-O

1 (6 oz.) package strawberry Jell-O

1 (3 oz.) package strawberry Jell-O

2 cups boiling water

1 cup cold water

1 (18 oz.) can crushed pineapple, not drained

2 bananas, mashed

2 (10 oz.) boxes frozen strawberries

2 cups sour cream

Dissolve Jell-O in boiling water, stir well. Add frozen strawberries, stir until thawed, add cold water, and pineapple; stir. Refrigerate until slightly thickened, about the consistency of egg whites. Add mashed bananas; pour half the mixture into a 9×13″ or 10×10 dish, refrigerate until firm. Leave the remaining mixture at room temperature. When Jell-O in dish is firm; spread sour cream over top, then spoon remaining Jell-O over sour cream. Refrigerate until firm.

Yield: 15 servings

Recipe from: Audrey Shriver Scalzo

*To reduce fat grams and calories. substitute reduced or fat-free sour cream.

Cal	Prot	Fat	Carb	Fiber	Chol	Sodium
180kc	3g	7g	30g	1g	15mg	60mg

Rosemarina Salad

1 large can pineapple
1 large can mandarin oranges
½ box tiny macaroni, cook & drain
Drain juice and add 2 tblsp. flour,
½ cup sugar
1 egg

Cook till thickens, when cool mix with macaroni & fruit, ½ cup nuts and 1 large cool whip.

Cal	Prot	Fat	Carb	Fiber	Chol	Sodium
160kc	2g	9g	19g	<1g	35mg	45mg

Rosemarina Salad (Revised)

Drain pineapple and oranges, set fruit aside. Combine flour and sugar in a small saucepan; add drained fruit juices and egg. Stirring with a wire whisk cook till mixture thickens, continue to cook about 2 minutes, remove from heat. Follow manufacturers directions to cook macaroni; drain well, mix with thickened sauce. Refrigerate several hours or overnight. Before serving; stir in fruit and gently fold in whipped topping.

Yield: 16 servings

*Use Soupettes, or Acine di Pepe if you can find them; or use orzo. They are all small macaroni products, but the first two work better.

Recipe from: Ginny Mangus

1 (20 oz.) can pineapple tidbits
1 (15 oz.) can mandarin oranges
½ box tiny macaroni*
3 tablespoons all-purpose flour
¼ cup + 2 tablespoons sugar
1 egg
dash salt
1 cup seedless grapes
1 banana, cut in chunks, optional
2 cups reduced-fat nondairy
  whipped topping

Cal	Prot	Fat	Carb	Fiber	Chol	Sodium
90kc	1g	2g	20g	0g	17mg	10mg

Salads

Chicken Salad

This is great for a light supper on a hot summer evening.

4 cups cubed cooked chicken
1 cup chopped celery
2 cups seedless grapes
½ teaspoon salt
½ teaspoon pepper
½ cup mayonnaise
½ cup sour cream
pecan halves, if desired
olives stuffed with pimento

Combine chicken, celery, grapes, salt & pepper. Toss lightly with mayonnaise and sour cream. May be served on lettuce, leaf, pineapple slice or cantaloupe ring. Garnish with pecan halves and olives.

Yield: 6 servings

Recipe from: Caroline Shriver

*To reduce fat grams and calories, substitute reduced-fat mayonnaise and reduced-fat sour cream.

Cal	Prot	Fat	Carb	Fiber	Chol	Sodium
360kc	28g	22g	11g	<1g	95mg	390mg

Salads

Corned Beef Salad

1 (3 oz) pkg lemon Jell-O
½ cup boiling water mix and
   cool;
1 cup mayonaize,(sic) with
   Jell-O
1 can corned beef crumbled
1 small onion chopped fine
3 hard boiled eggs chopped

There were no directions, other then what you see.

Recipe from: Eleanor Shriver

Cal	Prot	Fat	Carb	Fiber	Chol	Sodium
250kc	10g	20g	7g	0g	85mg	420mg

Corned Beef Salad (Revised)

Combine Jell-O and boiling water, stir to dissolve; refrigerate until thickened to consistency of egg whites. When thickened, add remaining ingredients and spoon into a 10×10″ 9×12″ pan. Chill until firm. To serve: Cut into squares and place on a lettuce leaf on individual salad plates. Serve with warm rolls for lunch.

Yield: 12 servings

1 (6 oz) package lemon Jell-O
1½ cups boiling water
1 cup reduced-fat mayonnaise
1 (12 oz.) can corned beef,
   crumbled
½ cup finely chopped onion
½ cup finely chopped celery
2 hard boiled eggs, chopped
1 teaspoon Worcestershire sauce
2 tablespoons fresh lemon juice

Cal	Prot	Fat	Carb	Fiber	Chol	Sodium
210kc	10g	12g	15g	0g	60mg	510mg

Salads

SALAD DRESSINGS

Dressing

This dressing is good on all sorts of salads, Grandma Detar used to serve it on a lettuce salad, serve on any kind of vegetable or pasta salads.

3 tablespoon sugar
1 teaspoon cider vinegar
2 teaspoon yellow mustard
1 cup mayonnaise*

Mix together; chill.

Yield: 1¼ cups or 10 (2 tablespoon) servings

*To reduce fat substitute reduced-fat or fat-free mayonnaise.

Recipe from: Goldie Shaffer

Cal	Prot	Fat	Carb	Fiber	Chol	Sodium
105kc	0g	8g	27g	0g	116mg	222mg

Salad Dressing

Blend in blender. Especially good on fresh fruit.

Yield: 2½ cups or
20 (2 tablespoon) servings

Recipe from: Ruth Altmire

*To reduce calories substitute 6 packets of artificial sweetener, (1½ tsp) plus ¼ cup sugar.

⅔ cup sugar, can substitute
   honey*
1 tsp. salt
⅓ cup lemon juice
1 tblsp. yellow mustard
1 small onion
1 tsp. celery seed
dash pepper

Cal	Prot	Fat	Carb	Fiber	Chol	Sodium
130kc	0g	11g	8g	0g	0mg	125mg

Homemade Mayonaise (sic)

1 cup sugar
2 tblsp. flour
3 eggs
¾ cup vinegar
1½ cups milk

Cook until thick.

Cal	Prot	Fat	Carb	Fiber	Chol	Sodium
43kc	1g	1g	6g	0g	36mg	15mg

Homemade Mayonnaise (Revised)

Combine sugar and flour in a saucepan, add remaining ingredients, using a wire whisk. Cook over medium heat, stirring constantly with whisk until thick. Continue stirring with the wire whisk if mixture starts to curdle.

1 cup sugar
2 tablespoons all-purpose flour
2 eggs and ¼ cup egg substitute
½ cup vinegar
1½ cups reduced-fat milk*

Yield: 3 cups or 24 (2 tablespoon) servings

*Substitute ½ cup fat-free half-and-half for a smoother creamer consistency.

Cal	Prot	Fat	Carb	Fiber	Chol	Sodium
30kc	1g	.5g	5g	0g	23mg	10mg

Salads

Vegetarian

Macaroni & Cheese

1 to 1&½ cup uncooked elbow
  macaroni
¼ cup margarine
¼ cup chopped onion
½ tsp. salt
¼ tsp. pepper
¼ cup flour
1¾ cup milk
8 oz. cheese

Cook macaroni & drain. Cook margarine, onion, salt and pepper until onion is tender. Stir in flour. Cook until smooth and bubbly. Stir in milk. Heat to boiling, stirring constantly. Boil and stir 1 minute. Remove from heat. Layer macaroni and cheese in a greased deep casserole dish, in 2 layers. Pour milk mixture over top. Bake, uncovered, at 375 degrees for 30 min.

Cal	Prot	Fat	Carb	Fiber	Chol	Sodium
360kc	18g	22g	24g	<1g	45mg	570mg

Macaroni & Cheese (Revised)

Preheat oven to 350 degrees; spray a 2 quart casserole with vegetable spray.

Cook macaroni according to package directions; drain. Melt margarine in a medium size saucepan. Add onion, cook until tender, add salt and pepper. Using a quart jar combine flour and milk, shake to dissolve; gradually add to onion mixture, stirring constantly until mixture comes to a boil. Cook 1 minute while constantly stirring; remove from heat, add cheese; continue to stir until melted. Add macaroni and toss until combined, pour into prepared casserole. Combine Parmesan cheese and bread crumbs; sprinkle over top. Bake, uncovered, at 375 degrees for 30 min.

Yield: 6 servings

*Can substitute ½ cup of fat-free half-and-half for creamier consistency.

vegetable spray
1½ cup uncooked elbow
  macaroni
2 tablespoons margarine
¼ cup chopped onion
½ teaspoon salt
freshly ground black pepper,
  as desired
dash cayenne pepper
¼ cup all-purpose flour
1¾ cup reduced-fat milk*
1½ cups shredded
  reduced-fat cheddar
  cheese
¼ cup Parmesan cheese
¼ cup fine bread crumbs

Cal	Prot	Fat	Carb	Fiber	Chol	Sodium
260kc	17g	9g	27g	<1g	10mg	570mg

Enchilada Sauce

This recipe originally came from Betty Ciochetti Fleming who learned to make it from her mother, Mary Ciochetti. Common to the cooks of that era, Mary cooked by instinct, so Betty, by watching her mother, developed the following recipe. This recipe in turn was handed down from Betty to her daughter, Kathy Fleming, and passed on to my daughter-in-law, Angie Ciochetti Shriver. Kathy said, "My mom used to make cheese enchiladas on Friday nights, (in those days, Catholics did not eat meat on Fridays, remember!) Enchilada night became a neighborhood tradition, with everybody getting into the act of rolling up enchiladas. My mom always shared the recipe with anybody who asked, but no one has ever made them quite as good as she did."

3–4 T. shortening
3–4 cloves garlic
2 T. flour
1 T. chili powder
1 can tomato sauce
1 can water
few drops vinegar
grated cheese
chopped onions
tortillas (corn)
chopped olives
cheese

Melt shortening & brown garlic in it. Remove browned garlic & remove pan from fire. Mix together flour & chili powder & add to shortening. Add tomato sauce, water & vinegar. Simmer a long time, till thick. Thin with olive juice. Add cheese before thinning. Dip lightly cooked tortillas in sauce. Put olives, onions & cheese in middle and roll up.

Recipe from: Betty Ciochetti Fleming

Cal	Prot	Fat	Carb	Fiber	Chol	Sodium
180kc	7g	11g	16g	2g	20mg	270mg

Enchilada Sauce & Cheese Enchiladas (Revised)

2 tablespoons olive oil
4 cloves garlic
2 tablespoons all-purpose flour
1 tablespoon chili powder
1 (8 oz.) can tomato sauce
1 (8 oz.) can water
¼ teaspoon vinegar
vegetable spray
8 ounces reduced fat or fat-free
mild cheese, divided
½ cup chopped onions
1 (2½ oz.) can chopped olives
12 corn tortillas

Heat oil in a large skillet or sauce pan; add garlic and cook on medium-low until brown. Remove browned garlic; discard or save for another use.* Remove skillet from heat. Blend flour and chili powder; add to oil, stirring constantly until smooth. Add tomato sauce, water and vinegar, cook over medium heat, uncovered, until thick, it should be about the consistency of a creamed soup.** Drain olives, reserve olives. Thin enchilada sauce with olive liquids as needed.

Preheat oven to 350 degrees; spray a 10″ baking dish with vegetable spray.

Add about ¼ cup cheese; stir until melted. Dip tortillas in enchilada sauce; lay on plate. Place about 2 tablespoons cheese, 1 tablespoon olives, and ½ tablespoon onions in middle of tortilla and roll up, place in prepared baking dish, pour remaining sauce over all. Bake in 350 degree oven about 30 minutes or until cheese melts and they are heated through.

Serve with lettuce and tomato salad, and baked tortilla chips.

Yield: 12 enchiladas or 4 servings

*The cooked garlic is great added to mashed potatoes.
**Sauce can be prepared days ahead.

This dish can also be prepared as a casserole layering the dipped tortillas, then olives, onions, and cheese. Repeat until all ingredients are used, ending with cheese.

Cal	Prot	Fat	Carb	Fiber	Chol	Sodium
150kc	7g	7g	17g	2g	10mg	310mg

Poultry

Chicken Cordon Bleu

4 chicken breast halves, boned
  & skinned
4 thin slices Prosciutto ham
4 thin slices Swiss cheese
2 eggs
1 cup bread crumbs
clarified butter

Pound chicken into cutlets about ¼″ thick. Salt & pepper; lay one slice ham and one slice cheese on each chicken breast, roll as for a jelly roll, tucking in sides. Press ends to seal well, tie with #8 string. Dip in eggs then in bread crumbs, coating well. Let stand about 10 minutes. Sauté in clarified butter until brown on each side and tender.

Cal	Prot	Fat	Carb	Fiber	Chol	Sodium
558kc	71g	22g	22g	<1g	291mg	1080mg

Chicken Cordon Bleu (Revised)

Preheat oven to 400 degrees; spray a broiler pan & rack with vegetable spray.

Place chicken pieces between two pieces of clear plastic wrap. Pound to form cutlets about ¼″ thick. Sprinkle with pepper. Place a ham slice on top of chicken, top with cheese slice, roll meat as for jelly roll, tucking in sides. Press end to seal well, secure with a wooden pick. Combine cornflake, bread crumbs, and paprika. Dip chicken rolls into beaten eggs, then roll in crumbs to coat well. Place on prepared broiler pan, carefully spray with vegetable spray for 2 seconds. Bake in 400 degree oven, uncovered, for 45–55 minutes or until tender.

vegetable spray
4 boneless, skinless chicken
  breast halves
4 thin slices reduced fat ham
  or Prosciutto ham
4 thin slices Swiss cheese
2 egg whites +1 whole egg,
  beaten
1 cup cornflake crumbs
½ cup fine bread crumbs
¼ teaspoon paprika

Yield: 4 servings

Recipe from: Evelena Barbutes

Cal	Prot	Fat	Carb	Fiber	Chol	Sodium
490kc	69g	15g	17g	0g	180mg	960mg

Chicken & Dumplings

Chicken and dumplings was another of my mom's special meals. She would always coat her dumplings well with the excess flour; this helped thicken the broth. Then she would serve them with mashed potatoes, green peas, and cranberries or coleslaw.

stewing chicken
salt & pepper
2 cups flour
4 tsp. baking powder
2 tblsp. Crisco shortening

Cut chicken in pieces, salt & pepper; cover with water and cook slow till tender. Bone chicken and strip from bones; return to hot broth.

Make dumplings: Sift flour, salt, and baking powder, cut shortening into flour. Add milk, stir carefully. Roll out to about ¼" thick on floured board, cut into small squares, coat good with extra flour. Drop into boiling broth. Cover, boil 12 minutes or until dumplings are done. Don't lift lid for at least 10 minutes.

Recipe from: Oma Day

Cal	Prot	Fat	Carb	Fiber	Chol	Sodium
387kc	57g	15g	35g	1g	65mg	341mg

Chicken & Dumplings (Revised)

Place chicken in a wide-top soup kettle. Add salt, pepper, thyme, and sage, cover with water. *If you are using chicken breast, at this time add a small bouillon cube. Bring to a boil; reduce heat and continue to cook on low heat until tender. Remove chicken from broth; skim fat from broth and discard; remove meat from bones and return meat to broth. Bring broth and meat to a gentle boil. While this is coming to a boil, make dumplings: Combine baking mix and milk, using a fork to gently blend. **Roll out on a floured surface to about ¼"

| 1 whole chicken, cut into pieces or 4 chicken breast halves* |
| salt and black pepper to taste |
| 1 teaspoon thyme |
| ½ teaspoon ground sage |
| 1¾ cups reduced-fat baking mix*** |
| ⅔ cups reduced-fat milk |

thickness. Using a table-knife, cut in about ¾" squares. Gently toss these around in the flour to coat. This makes the broth good and thick. Carefully drop into simmering broth, continuing until all the dough is used. Be careful not to overcrowd dumplings in the pot. Immediately cover the pot and steam dumplings 12 minutes, remove cover and cook 10 minutes or until dumplings are done. Test the dumplings with a wooden pick, if the pick comes out clean, they are done.

Yield: 6 servings

**To make drop dumplings, dip a teaspoon into hot broth first; then take a teaspoon full of batter and drop into boiling broth, continue as above.
***You can use baking mix for dumplings or use Isabelle's Fluffy Dumplings, page 21.

Cal	Prot	Fat	Carb	Fiber	Chol	Sodium
340kc	40g	6g	26g	<1g	100mg	500mg

Poultry

Fried Chicken

I know a lot of people say this, but, honestly, my mom made the very best fried chicken ever!!! She would serve it with a number of different things, but my favorite was mashed potatoes, green beans, coleslaw, and biscuits. Yum, yum!

1 large frying chicken
salt, pepper, and flour
vegetable oil
milk

Cut chicken into pieces, sprinkle salt and pepper over and rub in. Roll in flour. Have oil good and hot. (My mom used a large iron skillet with cover, which she called a chicken fryer!) Add chicken, brown quickly, lower heat; cover and cook on low heat till tender, about 20–25 minutes. Take lid off, turn heat up and cook a few minutes more until coating is crispy. Put chicken on platter. Pour off grease except for about 2 tablespoons, add about ¼ cup of flour, cook over medium heat till nice and brown and bubbly. Pour about 2 cups milk, diluted a little with water, into flour and stir real good to work out all the lumps. When bubbly and thick, add salt & pepper to taste.

Recipe from: Oma Day

Cal	Prot	Fat	Carb	Fiber	Chol	Sodium
280kc	30g	16g	3g	0g	95mg	90mg

I am convinced the reason our foremothers had such great iron skillets was because they fried almost everything they ate , thus keeping them well-seasoned.

See page 237 for helpful hints in caring for your iron skillet.

I will admit that nothing can replace Mom's fried chicken. However, I have found a few alternatives that are not so loaded with fat and cholesterol. Following is one my family enjoys.

Almost Fried Chicken (Revised)

vegetable spray
4 boneless, skinless chicken
    breast halves
1 cup crushed cornflakes
¼ teaspoon paprika
1 egg, slightly beaten
½ cup milk
½ cup + 2 tablespoons
    all-purpose flour
salt and black pepper to taste
1 cup chicken broth
¼ cup water

Preheat oven to 400 degrees; spray broiler pan and rack with vegetable spray.

Slightly dry chicken pieces with paper towel, set aside. Combine cornflake crumbs and paprika; set aside. In a small bowl slightly beat egg, milk, ¼ teaspoon salt and black pepper as desired. Gradually add ½ cup flour, beating constantly with a wire whisk until mixture is smooth. Dip each piece of chicken into batter; after excess has dripped off, roll in cornflake crumbs and place on prepared broiler pan. Carefully spray chicken with vegetable spray for about 2 seconds. Bake in 400 degree oven, uncovered, for about 35–40 minutes or until tender.

While chicken is baking: Bring chicken broth to a gentle boil. Combine remaining 2 tablespoons flour with ¼ cup water, stir until very smooth. While stirring, slowly add flour mixture to simmering broth; continue to stir until mixture thickens. Add salt and black pepper to taste. Serve over mashed potatoes or hot biscuits.

Yield: 4–6 servings

Cal	Prot	Fat	Carb	Fiber	Chol	Sodium
290kc	42g	6g	15g	0g	130mg	340mg

Poultry

Chicken Kiev

fat for frying

4 whole chicken breast halved,
    boned, skinned

salt & pepper

2 tablespoons chopped green
    onion

4 tablespoons chives

12 tablespoons butter

2 eggs, beaten

2 tablespoons milk

1 cup bread crumbs

Recipe from: Judy Morris

Place chicken pieces between two pieces of clear plastic wrap. Pound to form cutlets about ¼" thick. Sprinkle with salt & pepper, onion & chives. Cut chilled butter into 1½ tablespoon pieces; place at end of each cutlet. Roll meat as for jelly roll, tucking in sides. Press end to seal well, roll with #8 thread. Coat each roll with bread crumbs, then in egg mixture and again in bread crumbs; coat well. Chill thoroughly at least 1 hour. Fry chicken rolls in deep hot fat (375 degrees) about 8–10 minutes.

Yield: 8 servings

Cal	Prot	Fat	Carb	Fiber	Chol	Sodium
345kc	31g	23g	10g	0g	191mg	168mg

Chicken Kiev (Revised)

Preheat oven to 400 degrees; spray broiler pan and rack with vegetable spray.

Place chicken pieces between two pieces of clear plastic wrap. Pound to form cutlets about ¼" thick. Sprinkle with salt, pepper, green onion and chives. Divide very cold butter, form into 4 slender rolls, place rolls at the end of each cutlet. Roll meat as for jelly roll, tucking in sides. Press end to seal well, secure with a wooden pick. Combine egg whites and milk; set aside. Combine bread crumbs, Parmesan cheese, and Italian seasoning. Dip chicken rolls in egg mixture then into crumbs; place on prepared broiler pan, carefully spray with vegetable spray for about 2 seconds. Bake in 400 degree oven, uncovered, for 35–45 minutes or until tender.

Yield: 4 servings

vegetable spray

4 boneless, skinless, chicken
    breast halves

¼ teaspoon salt

freshly ground black pepper

2 tablespoons chopped green
    onion

4 tablespoons chopped chives

4 teaspoons butter

2 egg whites, or ½ cup egg
    substitute, beaten

2 tablespoons reduced-fat milk

1 cup fine, dry bread crumbs

¼ cup Parmesan cheese

½ teaspoon Italian seasoning

Cal	Prot	Fat	Carb	Fiber	Chol	Sodium
256kc	31g	14g	21g	<1g	64mg	336mg

Poultry

y traditional Thanksgiving menu is a blending of my mom's and Mom Shriver's traditional dishes. I normally serve:

Fresh fruit salad
Roast Turkey
Bread stuffing
Corn bread dressing, page 22
Gravy
Mashed potatoes, page 143
Candied sweet potatoes, page 142
Steamed broccoli
Succotash, page 135
Cranberries or cranberry salad, page 42
*Saltine crackers**
Dinner rolls, page 10
Pumpkin pie, page 169
Pecan Pie
Assortment of cookies

*The Shrivers always served crackers with this type of meal. They would crumble the crackers in large crumbs alongside the mashed potatoes and spoon gravy over crackers and potatoes.

Poultry

Roasted Poultry

I basically use the same method for either chicken or turkey, the only difference is the amount of time they bake.

1 turkey or roasting chicken
salt and pepper as desired
prepared stuffing*
cooking oil
cheese cloth

Preheat oven to 450 degrees; spray roasting pan and rack with vegetable spray.

Wash and drain turkey. If desired, rub inside cavity with salt and pepper. Place prepared stuffing in cavity and secure loosely with metal skewers. Place bird on rack in a roasting pan; cover with cheese cloth, drizzle oil over all. Place in preheated 450 degree oven; reduce heat to 350 degrees. Bake, basting frequently, until meat thermometer inserted in thickest part registers 180–185 degrees, or allow 20–25 minutes per pound for small birds up to 6 pounds, for larger birds, allow 15–20 minutes.

*Stuffing: At the Shriver's, the night before the holiday meal, Mom Shriver would spread sliced bread on the counter to dry out. Next morning, the children would be permitted to break the bread into large crumbs, which they always turned into a fun job. Next Mom would add sautéed diced celery and onions, salt, pepper, sage, thyme, butter, and broth; after mixing thoroughly, she would stuff it into the chicken. Dad preferred dry stuffing, so Mom would always save some of the stuffing out, this she would place in a muslin cloth bag and heat it the last few minutes before dinner was served. I find that today there are many good stuffing mix products on the market which my family likes, so I do take the easy way out. For years this was the only stuffing I made because I could not master my mother's method of making corn bread dressing, but as I said earlier in this book, I finally mastered a recipe I really like, so I make both regular stuffing and corn bread dressing. See page 22 for corn bread dressing.

Poultry

Chicken Pot Pie

My mom made chicken pot pie fairly often, but more so after a holiday when she had leftover chicken or turkey.

> 3 cups cooked chicken or turkey, diced
> potato, carrots, peas, celery and onions, diced
> flour, salt, & pepper
> biscuits

Cook vegetables until tender, add chicken. Mix flour with a little water, stir till smooth. Slowly add to gently boiling vegetable mixture; stir until slightly thickened. Pour into baking dish, top with biscuits. Bake in 400 degree oven until brown.

Cal	Prot	Fat	Carb	Fiber	Chol	Sodium
260kc	17g	5g	42g	4g	28mg	906mg

Recipe from: Oma Day

Chicken Pot Pie (Revised)

Cook carrots, onion, celery, and lima beans in boiling water to cover, about 10 minutes, add potatoes and continue to cook until tender, about 20 minutes. Add peas, cook 4–5 minutes. While peas are cooking, combine water and flour in a jar; shake until smooth. Gradually add to hot vegetable mixture, stirring constantly until slightly thickened. Add bouillon, poultry seasoning, salt, pepper, and chicken, heat thoroughly.

While vegetables are cooking preheat oven to 450 degrees; spray a 10×10″ or 9×13″ casserole with vegetable spray. Pour chicken/vegetable mixture into prepared casserole. Combine baking mix and milk, gently blending with a fork. Place on lightly floured surface, knead a few times. Roll dough about ¼–⅓″ thick, cut with biscuit cutter or small glass dipped in flour. Place over chicken/vegetable mixture.* Place in 450 degree oven, bake 7–9 minutes or until biscuits are nicely browned.

Yield: 8 servings

*Substitute 3 cups frozen mixed vegetables if desired

> 2 carrots, diced*
> ½ cup chopped onion
> ½ cup chopped celery
> 1 cup lima beans*
> 1 large potato, diced*
> ½ cup frozen peas*
> ¼ teaspoon poultry seasoning, according to taste
> ½ teaspoon salt, or more to taste
> freshly ground black pepper
> ½ cup water
> 2 tablespoons all-purpose flour
> 2 teaspoons granular chicken bouillon
> 3 cups cooked chicken or turkey, diced
> 2 cups reduced-fat baking mix
> ¾ cup reduced-fat milk

Cal	Prot	Fat	Carb	Fiber	Chol	Sodium
260kc	17g	3.5g	40g	4g	30mg	790mg

Cooking with Grandma and the Girls

Poultry

Overnight Chicken Casserole

2 cups diced cooked chicken
2 cups raw macaroni
2 cans mushroom soup
1 soup can milk
1 small onion, chopped
1 can chicken broth
½ green pepper, chopped
1 small jar pimentos, diced
1 can sliced water chestnuts
½ lb. grated cheddar cheese
½ teaspoon salt

Mix all together. Pour into well greased baking dish, refrigerate overnight. 350 degrees, 1 hour.

Cal	Prot	Fat	Carb	Fiber	Chol	Sodium
390kc	28g	18g	29g	2g	60mg	1220mg

Overnight Chicken Casserole (Revised)

Spray a 9×13 pan with vegetable spray. Layer all ingredients in the following order: Spread raw noodles in bottom of pan, spread chicken over noodles. Distribute onion, green pepper, pimentos, water chestnuts and fat-free cheese evenly over noodles and chicken. In a small bowl combine soup, milk and broth, pour over mixture in pan. No need to stir. Sprinkle with the remaining ¼ lb. reduced-fat cheese. Cover with foil and refrigerate at least 8 hours. When ready to cook; preheat oven to 350 degrees. Remove foil and bake 1 hour or until most of the liquid is absorbed.

Yield: 8 servings

*When I am incorporating cheese into a dish, I use fat-free cheese because it will melt very well when mixed with other ingredients. However, if the cheese is to be sprinkled on top, I use reduced-fat because fat-free doesn't melt very well, it just becomes rubbery.

2 cups raw noodles
2 cups cooked chicken, chopped
1 small onion, chopped
¼ cup chopped green pepper
1 (2 oz.) jar pimentos, diced and drained
1 (5 oz.) can sliced water chestnuts, drained
¼ lb. grated fat-free sharp cheddar cheese*
2 (10 ¾ oz.) cans low-fat, low-sodium condensed cream of mushroom soup
1 soup can reduced-fat milk
1½ cups low-fat, low-sodium chicken broth
¼ lb. grated reduced-fat cheddar cheese*

Cal	Prot	Fat	Carb	Fiber	Chol	Sodium
290kc	24g	6g	33g	2g	35mg	760mg

Turkey Noodle Casserole

1 package or 2 cups cooked wide
    noodles
3 cups cooked turkey
1 can cream of chicken soup
½ cup milk
½ cup chopped green peppers
½ cup chopped green onions
3 tablespoons butter
1 small can mushrooms
1 (12 oz.) cottage cheese
12 oz. shredded Cheddar cheese
½ cup Parmesan cheese
salt to taste

Sauté peppers and onion in butter. Mix all ingredients together except the Parmesan cheese. Pour into a greased 9×13 pan; sprinkle with Parmesan cheese. Bake until bubbly at 350 degrees. You can use chicken instead, if you like.

Cal	Prot	Fat	Carb	Fiber	Chol	Sodium
710kc	50g	42g	32g	2g	155mg	1340mg

Turkey Noodle Casserole (Revised)

Preheat oven to 350 degrees; spray a 10×10 baking dish with vegetable spray.

Cook noodles according to package directions; drain. Heat olive oil in a nonstick skillet; add peppers, onions, and mushrooms, sauté until tender. Combine noodles, vegetable mixture, turkey, cottage cheese, and cheddar cheese; spoon into prepared baking dish, sprinkle with Parmesan cheese. Bake in 350 degree oven for 30 minutes.

Yield: 6 servings

*Chicken can be substituted for turkey.

Serve with a green vegetable and applesauce.

vegetable spray
2 cups raw noodles
3 cups cooked turkey, cubed*
1 (10 ¾ oz.) can low-fat,
    low-sodium condensed cream
    of chicken soup
½ cup reduced-fat milk
1 teaspoon olive oil
⅓ cup chopped green peppers
⅓ cup chopped green onions
1 cup sliced fresh mushrooms
1 cup fat-free cottage cheese
8 oz. shredded fat-free sharp
    Cheddar cheese
½ cup Parmesan cheese

Cal	Prot	Fat	Carb	Fiber	Chol	Sodium
480kc	43g	15g	39g	2g	80mg	870mg

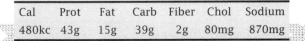

Hot Chicken Casserole

4 chicken breast, cooked and cut
into chunks

1 cup thinly sliced celery

mayonnaise, enough to moisten

1 tblsp. lemon juice

½ small can sliced mushrooms

2 tsps. minced onion

¼ tsp. salt

dash pepper

Cheddar cheese

potato chips

Hours before or night before combine all the above ingredients; toss lightly. Place in refrigerator until baking time. Before baking: Sprinkle 4 oz. grated Cheddar cheese over all, top with a layer of crushed potato chips. Bake in 350 degree oven 20 minutes covered, then 5 minutes uncovered. DON'T OVERBAKE!

Yield: 4–5 servings

Cal	Prot	Fat	Carb	Fiber	Chol	Sodium
748kc	64g	41g	30g	1g	190mg	1010mg

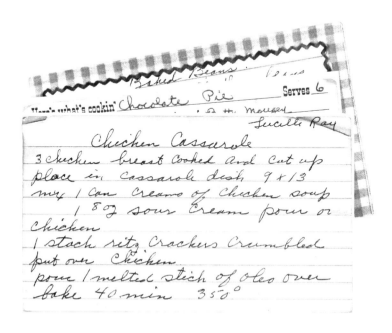

Chicken Casserole

3 chicken breast cooked and cut up
place in casserole dish 9 x 13
mix 1 can cream of chicken soup
1 8 oz sour cream pour on
chicken
1 stack ritz crackers crumbled
put over chicken
pour 1 melted stick of oleo over
bake 40 min 350°

Hot Chicken Casserole (Revised)

This is great when you are having friends in for lunch. You can prepare it ahead of time and bake when needed.

vegetable spray
8 boneless, skinless, chicken
    breast halves
½ teaspoon thyme
¼ cup dry white wine
1 carrot, cut into chunks
1 stalk of celery, cut into
    chunks +1 cup thinly diced
½ small onion, cut into
    quarters +¼ cup chopped
    onion
½ cup fresh mushrooms,
    sliced
1 (2 oz.) jar chopped pimentos
¾ cup reduced-fat mayonnaise
    (enough to moisten)
1 tablespoon lemon juice
½ teaspoon salt
dash pepper
4 ounces reduced-fat sharp
    Cheddar cheese
1½ cups course bread crumbs

Day before or hours before; cook chicken in wine, thyme, carrot and celery chunks, onion quarters, and enough water to cover chicken. Bring to a boil, reduce heat to simmer; cook for about 1½ hours, until very tender. Drain chicken, cool and cut into cubes. Discard vegetables; reserve broth for use another time. In a large mixing bowl combine chicken, mushrooms, pimentos, and remaining celery and onion. In a small bowl combine mayonnaise, lemon juice, salt, and pepper; add to chicken, toss lightly. Spoon into a 10×10″ baking dish which has been sprayed with vegetable spray; place in refrigerator until baking time. Remove from refrigerator 30 minutes before baking; sprinkle cheddar cheese over all, top with a layer of bread crumbs. Carefully spray bread crumbs with vegetable spray for about 2 seconds.

Bake in a preheated 350 degree oven 20 minutes covered, then 5 minutes uncovered. DON'T OVERBAKE!

Yield: 8 servings

Cal	Prot	Fat	Carb	Fiber	Chol	Sodium
275kc	61g	11g	21g	2g	90mg	477mg

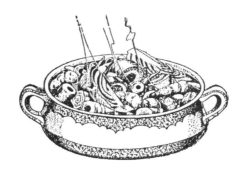

Chicken and Egg Salad Casserole

2–4 cups cooked chicken cubed
1 cup celery sliced thin
4 hard cooked eggs
1 can water chestnuts, sliced
1 can cream of chicken soup
1 tsp. minced onion
1 tsp. lemon juice
¾ cup Marzetti slaw dressing
1 cup rice cooked
1 tsp. salt

Combine above ingredients. Place in buttered casserole. Bake 35–40 min. at 350 degrees. Remove from oven before baking time expires and add: (I think you should return it to oven for 5–10 minutes to brown.)

1 cup corn flake crumbs
⅛ cup melted butter
½ cup slivered almonds

(No directions for this.)

Cal	Prot	Fat	Carb	Fiber	Chol	Sodium
530kc	36g	28g	34g	3g	225mg	1240mg

Chicken and Egg Salad Casserole (Revised)

6 boneless, skinless, chicken
   breast halves
½ teaspoon thyme
¼ cup dry white wine
1 carrot, cut into chunks
1 stalk of celery, cut into chunks
   +1 cup thinly diced
½ small onion, cut into quarters
   +¼ cup diced onion
2 hard cooked eggs, sliced
1 can water chestnuts, sliced
1 cup cooked rice
1 (10 ¾ oz.) can low-fat,
   low-sodium condensed cream
   of chicken soup
1 teaspoon lemon juice
¾ cup reduced-fat mayonnaise
¼ cup skim milk
1 teaspoon vinegar
1 tablespoon sugar
1 cup cornflake crumbs
2 teaspoons melted margarine
2 tablespoons almond slivers

Cook chicken in wine, thyme, carrot and celery chunks, onion quarters, and enough water to cover chicken. Bring to a boil, reduce heat to simmer, cook for about 1 hour, until very tender. Drain chicken, cool and cut into cubes. Discard vegetables; reserve broth to use another time.

Preheat oven to 350 degrees; spray baking dish with vegetable spray.

Combine chicken, remaining celery and onions, eggs, chestnuts, and rice in a large mixing bowl. In a small bowl combine soup, lemon juice, mayonnaise, milk, vinegar, and sugar, pour over chicken mixture; blend well. Spoon into prepared baking dish, bake in 350 degree oven for 20 minutes. Combine cornflake crumbs, margarine and almond slivers; crumble over chicken mixture. Continue baking until heated through and top is brown.

Yield: 6 servings

Poultry

Cal	Prot	Fat	Carb	Fiber	Chol	Sodium
304kc	30g	12g	7g	2g	107mg	640mg

Pork

Pork

Ham Loaf

1½ lb. ham, ground
½ lb. pork, ground
2 eggs
1 onion
¾ cup milk
¼ cup catsup
Broth:
½ cup brown sugar
2 tsp. dry mustard
¼ cup water
¼ cup vinegar

There were no directions for this recipe.

Recipe from: Pearl Held

Cal	Prot	Fat	Carb	Fiber	Chol	Sodium
490kc	33g	28g	26g	<1g	160mg	1250mg

Ham Loaf (Revised)

Preheat oven to 350 degrees; spray loaf pan with vegetable spray. Combine ham, sausage, bread crumbs, pepper, eggs, and milk; spoon into prepared pan. Bring broth ingredients to a boil, pour over ham loaf, bake 1½ hours at 350 degrees.

Yield: 6 servings

Serve with scalloped potatoes and coleslaw, page 43.

1 lb. ground reduced-fat, reduced-sodium ham
½ lb. ground turkey sausage
1 cup bread crumbs
dash pepper
1 egg + 2 egg whites
2 tablespoons reduced-fat milk
1 cup brown sugar
1 teaspoon yellow mustard
½ cup water
½ cup vinegar

Cal	Prot	Fat	Carb	Fiber	Chol	Sodium
410kc	27g	10g	52g	0g	105mg	1170mg

Cooking with Grandma and the Girls

Ham & Macaroni Casserole

1½ cups elbow macaroni
1 can cream of mushroom
    soup
1 can whole kernel corn
1 cup cubed American cheese
1 cup cubed ham

Cook macaroni in salted water; drain, add remaining ingredients. Pour into greased casserole, top with buttered bread crumbs. Bake in 350 degree oven for 40–50 minutes.

Cal	Prot	Fat	Carb	Fiber	Chol	Sodium
310kc	18g	14g	30g	2g	35mg	1190mg

Ham & Macaroni Casserole (Revised)

Cook macaroni according to package directions, (no need to add salt). While macaroni is cooking preheat oven to 350 degrees; spray a 1½ quart casserole with vegetable spray. Drain macaroni, return to cooking pan. Add soup, corn, cheese, and Canadian bacon, mix well; pour into prepared casserole. Top with bread crumbs, carefully spray crumbs with vegetable spray for about 2 seconds. Bake in 350 degree oven for 30 minutes.

Yield: 6 servings

1½ cups elbow macaroni
vegetable spray
1 (10 ¾ oz.) can low-fat,
    low-sodium condensed cream
    of mushroom soup
1 cup frozen whole kernel corn
1 cup shredded reduced-fat sharp
    cheddar cheese
1 cup cubed Canadian bacon
1 cup fresh, course, bread crumbs

Cal	Prot	Fat	Carb	Fiber	Chol	Sodium
240kc	13g	4g	38g	2g	5mg	610mg

Pork

Myrt's Ham Pot Pie

Pot pies are very popular among the people where John grew up in Apollo, Pennsylvania; owing to their German heritage I'm sure. Pot pie is described as squares of dough which are dropped into a pot of boiling broth and cooked with meat. You can also add potatoes and onions.

Broth:

½ cup ham broth

5 cups water

1 potato quartered & sliced

1 cup chopped ham

Dumplings:

1½ cup flour

½ tsp. salt

½ cup butter or margarine

¼ cup milk or more

Heat broth & water, add ham and potato; cook until potato is tender.

Cut butter into flour and salt, add milk & mix. Roll out on floured waxed paper to 16×16 square, cut into 2" squares. Add dumplings to broth and cook 15 minutes.

Recipe from: Eleanor Shriver

Cal	Prot	Fat	Carb	Fiber	Chol	Sodium
320kc	10g	18g	30g	1g	15mg	830mg

Myrt's Ham Pot Pie (Revised)

In a wide-top pan, bring broth and water to a boil, add potato slices; bring to a boil, reduce heat and cook until tender; add ham. While potato is cooking, prepare dough for dumplings: Combine baking mix and milk, using a fork to gently blend. Roll out on a floured surface, to about ¼" thickness. Using a table knife, cut in about ¾" squares. Gently toss with the excess flour to coat; this thickens the broth nicely. Carefully drop into simmering broth, continuing until all the dough is used. Be careful not to overcrowd dumplings. Cover immediately; steam dumplings 12 minutes or until dumplings are done. (Don't lift lid for at least 10 minutes.) Remove cover and continue to cook 10 minutes more or until a wooden pick comes out clean.

½ cup ham broth

5 cups water

1 potato quartered and sliced thin

1 cup reduced-fat, reduced-sodium chopped ham

1⅔ cup reduced-fat baking mix

⅔ cup reduced-fat milk

Yield: 6 servings

**To make drop dumplings, dip a teaspoon into hot broth first; then take a teaspoon full of batter and drop into boiling broth, continue as above.

Cal	Prot	Fat	Carb	Fiber	Chol	Sodium
220kc	12g	4.5g	31g	<1g	20mg	840mg

Crispy Baked Pork Chops

6 pork chops
saltine crackers
1 egg
vegetable oil
salt & pepper to taste

Trim chops, crush crackers. Beat egg, add a little water. Dip chops in egg & water, then in cracker crumbs until coated good. Heat oil in a heavy skillet, add chops and cook until brown on both sides. Put in a baking pan, add a little water, about 1 T. Cover with foil and bake in medium oven for about 50 minutes. Remove foil and bake about 10 minutes more to crispen the chops.

Recipe from: Betty Mougey

Cal	Prot	Fat	Carb	Fiber	Chol	Sodium
360kc	23g	25g	10g	0g	110mg	520mg

Crispy Baked Pork Chops (Revised)

Preheat oven to 350 degrees; spray a shallow baking dish with vegetable spray.

Combine egg and 1 tablespoon water in a shallow pan or saucer; place cracker crumbs on waxed paper. Heat ½ tablespoon oil in a large heavy skillet. Dip chops in egg mixture, then into crumbs, pressing down gently to coat thoroughly with crumbs. Add chops to hot oil, cook until brown on both sides, add oil as needed. Transfer to prepared baking dish; add about 1 tablespoon water; cover with aluminum foil. Bake in 350 degree oven for about 1 to 1¼ hours, or until tender. Remove foil the last 10 minutes for a crispy coating.

4 boneless pork loin chops
½ stack saltine crackers, crushed fine
1 egg, beaten
2 tablespoons water, divided
1 tablespoon olive oil, divided
½ teaspoon salt
freshly ground black pepper

Yield: 4 servings

Cal	Prot	Fat	Carb	Fiber	Chol	Sodium
250kc	24g	11g	10g	0g	110mg	520mg

Pork

Sara's Baked Pork Chops and Cabbage

Brown chops, arrange in casserole, put slice of onion on top, add thinly chopped cabbage. Simmer well and pour over just enough milk to cover the mixture. Bake at 350 covered, until cabbage is tender and chops well done, (about) 1 hour. Serve with baked potatoes.

Recipe from: Eleanor Shriver

Baked Pork Chops & Cabbage (Revised)

Preheat oven to 350 degrees; spray an 8×8″ baking dish with vegetable spray.

Heat oil in a non-stick skillet; trim all visible fat from chops, and brown on both sides in hot oil. Place chops in prepared baking dish; top with onion slices, cabbage, salt, and pepper. Pour about ¼ cup water and ½ cup milk over all; cover. Bake in 350 degree oven 50–60 minutes or until chops and cabbage are tender.

Yield: 4 servings

vegetable spray
2 teaspoons olive oil
4 medium pork loin chops
½ medium onion, sliced
½ head cabbage, thinly sliced, approximately 4 cups
½ cup reduced-fat milk
½ teaspoon salt
⅛ or less black pepper

Cal	Prot	Fat	Carb	Fiber	Chol	Sodium
220kc	24g	10g	8g	2g	70mg	360mg

Chalupa

3 lb. pork loin roast
2 cloves garlic, chopped
2 tablespoons chili powder
1 small can chopped green
    chilies
1 lb. pinto beans
1 tablespoon ground cumin
    seed
1 teaspoon oregano
2 tablespoons salt

Cover beans with water, bring to boil. Boil 5 minutes; remove from heat and cover. Let stand 1 hour. Put everything else in pan with beans. Cook 6 hours, keep adding water as necessary. After 6 hours, remove pork roast and take out bones and break up meat. Return meat to pot. Cook with lid off one hour or until mixture is thick.

Recipe from: Pat Ciochetti

Cal	Prot	Fat	Carb	Fiber	Chol	Sodium
340kc	34g	17g	11g	4g	95mg	1280mg

Chalupa (Revised)

Place beans in a large soup pot, cover beans with water, bring to boil. Cook for 5 minutes; remove from heat and cover. Let stand 1 hour. Add garlic, chili powder, green chilies, cumin seed, oregano, and salt to pot with beans. Cook 6 hours; keep adding water as necessary. After 6 hours, remove pork roast; debone and break up meat, return to pot. Cook with lid off one hour or until mixture is thick.

Serve by rolling meat/bean mixture in a warm flour tortilla, roll; garnish with lettuce, chopped tomato, shredded cheese, sour cream, etc.

Yield: 10–12 servings

3 lb. pork loin roast, all
    visible fat removed
2 cloves garlic, chopped
2 tablespoons chili powder
1 (14 oz.) can chopped green
    chilies
1 lb. pinto beans, dry
1 tablespoon ground cumin
1 teaspoon oregano
1½ tablespoons salt

Cal	Prot	Fat	Carb	Fiber	Chol	Sodium
300kc	36g	11g	12g	5g	90mg	1070mg

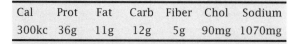

The traditional New Year's Day menu in the Shriver household started with pork roast and sauerkraut, served with mashed potatoes, homemade apple sauce, fresh dinner rolls, and some sort of vegetable. This is by far the simplest holiday meal to prepare.

Mom Shriver taught me this simple method of preparing pork and sauerkraut.

Pork Roast & Sauerkraut

pork roast
salt
sauerkraut

Bake salted pork in little water till almost done, add kraut and little water, cook till meat & kraut are tender.

Recipe from: Eleanor Shriver

Pork Roast & Sauerkraut (Revised)

vegetable spray
3 lb. very lean pork loin
½ teaspoon salt
freshly ground black pepper
1 quart sauerkraut

Preheat oven to 350 degrees. Spray roasting pan with spray. Place pork in pan, add salt, pepper and enough water to almost cover,. Bake about 1 hour, spoon sauerkraut all around the meat and add about 1 cup water or enough to make it juicy. Continue to bake 45–50 minutes or until meat is tender.

Yield: 9 servings

Cal	Prot	Fat	Carb	Fiber	Chol	Sodium
327kc	44g	9g	2g	1.6g	122mg	597mg

My mom, being true to her southern traditions, always served black-eyed peas with the New Year's meal and we frequently had lazy daisy cake. See page 189.

Hunter's Dinner
¼ lb dried lima beans
¾ lb lean pork
1 tablespoon bacon drippings (or butter)
1 medium onion
2½ teaspoons salt
2 branches celery
2 medium carrots
No 2 can tomatoes
1 green pepper
1 cup dried noodles & 1 tablespoon finely chopped parsley

Hunter's Dinner

¼ lb dried lima beans

¾ lean pork

1 tablespoon bacon drippings

1 medium onion

2 ½ teaspoon salt

2 branches celery

2 medium carrots

2 can tomatoes

1 green pepper

1 cup dried noodles & 1 tablespoon finely chopped parsley

Soak beans in 1 qt. cold water 3–4 hours. Cut pork into ½ inch cubes & brown in drippings with the chopped onion in a Dutch oven. Add the drained soaked beans, 3 cups of water and the salt, cover and simmer half an hour. Then add coarsely cut celery, thickly sliced carrots, the tomatoes & pepper & heat to boiling. Then add noodles. Again cover & cook 15 minutes, or until noodles are well cooked. Serve hot with parsley sprinkled over the top.

Recipe from: Eleanor Shriver

Cal	Prot	Fat	Carb	Fiber	Chol	Sodium
270kc	22g	8g	28g	5g	50mg	1140mg

Hunter's Dinner (Revised)

Trim fat from chops, cut into cubes. Heat oil in skillet, add loin cubes and onions; cook until browned. Add lima beans, celery, carrots, green pepper, tomatoes, salt, pepper, and 3 cups water. Bring to a gentle boil, reduce heat and simmer 35–40 minutes. Add noodles; cook 15 minutes or until noodles are tender. Sprinkle parsley over all.

Yield: 6 servings

This is a perfect dish for an electric skillet, use it as a one dish meal. Brown pork cubes and onions in it, proceed as directed above.

*Chicken is also good in this recipe.

2–3 pork loin chops*

2 teaspoons olive oil

1 small onion, chopped

one 10 oz. box frozen lima
beans

2 stalks celery, sliced

2 medium carrots, sliced

½ green pepper, chopped

1 (15 oz.) can tomatoes

¾ teaspoon salt

freshly ground black pepper

1 cup dried noodles

½ tablespoon finely chopped
parsley

Cal	Prot	Fat	Carb	Fiber	Chol	Sodium
220kc	15g	4g	34g	6g	20mg	440mg

Pork

Pork

I don't know to whom this "Sara" refers. S-A-R-A was a very common spelling in the Heckman-Detar family. As I mentioned earlier, John's mother's maiden name was Sara Elnora Detar, she had an aunt on her mother's side, Sara Jane Heckman and her maternal grandmother was Sara Schall, who married Abraham Heckman. One of our granddaughters was named Sara Elnora Scalzo after her great-grandmother Shriver.

Sara's Short Ribs

3 lb. short ribs
2 tsp. salt
½ cup chopped onion
½ cup water
1 clove garlic minced
6 oz tomato paste
1 cup catsup
¾ cup brown sugar
2 tblsp. prepared mustard
½ cup vinegar

Brown ribs on all sides in own fat. Cover and cook slowly 1 hr. Pour off drippings and add to meat the remaining mixture. Cover titely (sic) and cook for 1 ½ hr.

Recipe from: Eleanor Shriver

Cal	Prot	Fat	Carb	Fiber	Chol	Sodium
653kc	27g	51g	21g	1g	113mg	479mg

Sara's B-B-Q Ribs (Revised)

Spray a non-stick skillet with vegetable spray, when hot brown ribs on all sides. Cover; reduce heat to low and cook in its own juices slowly for 1 hour, adding a small amount water if necessary. While they are cooking: Combine remaining ingredients in a small saucepan; bring to a boil, reduce heat to simmer and cook 10–15 minutes.

Spray shallow baking pan with vegetable spray; preheat oven to 300 degrees.

Lift ribs from skillet with a slotted spoon, place in prepared baking pan, and discard meat juices. Pour sauce over ribs; cover, place in 300 degree oven and continue to cook for 1½ hours.

vegetable spray
3 lb. lean pork ribs*(much leaner than the beef short ribs)
½ teaspoon salt
½ cup water
½ cup vinegar
6 oz. tomato paste
1 cup catsup
¾ cup brown sugar
2 tablespoons prepared mustard
1 clove garlic minced
½ cup chopped onion

Yield: 10 servings

Cal	Prot	Fat	Carb	Fiber	Chol	Sodium
421kc	43g	18g	21g	1g	116mg	481mg

Beef

BEEF ENTREES

Mom Shriver loved to entertain; she enjoyed having people into their home and preparing large meals for them. Their dining room would be wall-to-wall table, and the table would be laden with food with 12 to 14 people seated around it wth the overflow of people (usually the children) finding a spot in the kitchen or on the front porch. There was never too many people, you could always find a spot somewhere.

Rump roast was one of Mom's favorite entrees. She would serve it with mashed potatoes, maybe green beans, a lime Jell-O salad, and either pie or cake (and sometimes both). You never left the Shriver's house hungry.

Mom didn't have a specific recipe, but I can share with you her method of cooking rump roast.

Rump Roast

Using a large heavy skillet, heat about 1 tablespoon of olive oil. When hot, carefully place the rump roast in the hot oil and sear it on each side. When all sides are brown, place in roasting pan, add about 1 cup water, cover and bake at 350 degrees until tender, maybe up to 3 hours, depending on size. Baste occasionally. Another method is to wrap roast in aluminum foil before placing in roasting pan. You can add salt and pepper after the roast has cooked or before.

Chuck Roast with Vegetables

This was a favorite of my mom's and mine. We never had a specific recipe, but I developed the following recipe in order to share this favorite meal with you.

vegetable spray
2 pound chuck roast,
    boneless, trimmed
¼ cup all-purpose flour
¼ teaspoon salt
pepper to taste
1 tablespoon olive oil
1½ cups water
3 large carrots
1 medium onion
3 medium potatoes

Preheat oven to 350 degrees: spray roasting pan with vegetable spray.

Trim all visible fat from chuck roast, dredge in flour, salt and pepper mixture. Heat oil in skillet, add roast and sear, top and bottom. When brown, place in prepared roasting pan; add water, cover and bake at 350 about 1¾ hours. While meat is cooking, prepare vegetables. Add peeled and quartered onion, carrots and potatoes; cook 50–60 minutes or until all is tender. Skim off and discard any visible fat. Add salt and pepper to vegetables to taste.

Yield: 8 servings

Serve this with cole slaw, page 43 and biscuits, page 9.

Cal	Prot	Fat	Carb	Fiber	Chol	Sodium
360kc	24g	20g	19g	2g	75mg	140mg

Beef

Swiss Steak

2 lb. round steak cut 1″ thick
1 tsp. salt
1 cup water
vegetable oil
flour
black pepper
1 small onion, chopped
1 cup canned tomatoes

Rub the salt and pepper into meat. Pound flour into steak, brown steak and onions in hot oil. Add water and tomatoes. Cover, simmer slowly until meat is tender.

Cal	Prot	Fat	Carb	Fiber	Chol	Sodium
508kc	39g	38g	2g	<1g	110mg	390mg

Swiss Steak (Revised)

Preheat oven to 325 degrees; spray a 9×13 baking dish with vegetable spray.

Cut steak into serving size pieces, pound flour into steak with a mallet, turn and repeat on other side, set aside. Heat 1 teaspoon oil in a large heavy skillet; when hot, add onion, pepper, celery and garlic; sauté but do not brown. Transfer to a small bowl and keep warm. Add remaining oil as needed to skillet, when hot add steak and cook until brown on both sides, repeat until all pieces are browned. Transfer meat to prepared baking dish, season with salt and pepper; spoon sautéed vegetables over meat, pour broth and tomatoes over all. Cover; bake in 325 degree oven for 2½ to 3 hours, or until tender.

vegetable spray
2 pounds top round steak
½ cup all-purpose flour
salt and black pepper to taste
2 tablespoons olive oil, divided
½ medium onion, sliced thin
½ green pepper, sliced thin
1 rib celery, sliced thin
1 clove garlic, minced
1 cup low-fat, low-sodium beef broth
1 cup canned tomatoes

Yield: 8 servings

Serve with mashed potatoes, noodles, or rice.

Cal	Prot	Fat	Carb	Fiber	Chol	Sodium
103kc	31g	8g	9g	<1g	100mg	149mg

Bavarian Beef Stew

1 lb. chuck beef

2 tblsp. fat

2 cups cold water

1 cup dry red wine

3 large onions, sliced

1 tsp. salt

1 tsp. pepper

1 tsp. paprika

8 whole cloves

3 tblsp. flour

1 recipe biscuits or dumplings

Cut the beef into small cubes and sear it in the fat until well browned. Cover the meat with water and wine, add onions. Let come to a boil and simmer for 2 hours. Add the salt, pepper, paprika and cloves, cook for another 20 minutes. Blend the flour with 2–3 tablespoons of stew liquid and stir the paste into the stew. Place biscuits on top, cover tightly and continue to cook until biscuits are done. You can use a recipe for dumplings instead, which is the real Bavarian way.

Yield: 6 servings

Cal	Prot	Fat	Carb	Fiber	Chol	Sodium
510kc	29g	21g	44g	3g	85mg	920mg

Beef

Bavarian Beef Stew (Revised)

1 lb. sirloin tip steak
½ teaspoon salt
⅛ teaspoon freshly ground
    black pepper
1 tablespoon olive oil
1½ cups tomato juice
½ cup dry red wine
1 bay leaf
¼ teaspoon paprika
2 whole cloves
1 small onion, cut into wedges
¼ cup sliced celery
3 small potatoes, cut into
    quarters
2 carrots, cut into chunks
1 tablespoon all-purpose flour
cold water
1 recipe biscuits, page 9 or 1
    recipe dumplings, page 21

Preheat oven to 350 degrees. Cut meat into bite size chunks, sprinkle with salt and pepper. Heat oil in a large skillet, add meat and brown. Lift meat into a large casserole, add tomato juice, wine, and bay leaf. Bake in 350 degree oven, covered, for 1½ hours. Add paprika, cloves, onion, celery, potatoes, and carrots. Cook about 45 minutes or until all vegetables are tender. Blend flour with 2–3 tablespoons cold water, stir into stew, stirring until thickened. Increase oven temperature to 400 degrees. Place biscuits on top of stew, return to oven and continue to bake about 10 minutes or until biscuits are golden brown. If you prefer dumplings instead of biscuits; at this point drop dumplings into simmering stew, cover and cook 10–12 minutes.

Yield: 6 servings

**This is a perfect dish for an electric skillet. If you have one, use it as a one-utensil dinner. Brown steak cubes in it, add juice, wine, bay leaf; reduce heat to 325 and cook as directed. Bake biscuits in oven on a baking sheet; when brown, split biscuit, place on individual plates and spoon stew over biscuits.

Cal	Prot	Fat	Carb	Fiber	Chol	Sodium
460kc	21g	15g	48g	3g	50mg	840mg

Corned Beef and Cabbage

3–4 lb. corned beef brisket
¼ lb. salt pork
3 carrots, cut in chunks
2–3 medium onions, quartered
cabbage wedges

Cover corned beef with boiling water, cook on simmer about 2 hours, add salt pork and cook about 1 to 2 hours or until tender. Lift out beef and salt pork; add carrots, onions and cabbage cook about 45 minutes or until tender.

Cal	Prot	Fat	Carb	Fiber	Chol	Sodium
410kc	23g	30g	12g	4g	85mg	360mg

Corned Beef and Cabbage (Revised)

Rinse brisket; put all ingredients into crock pot in order listed. Cover; cook on low for 12–24 hours, (high 7–10 hours) Push cabbage wedges down in liquid after 5–6 hours on low or 2–3 hours on high.*

Yield: 8–10 servings

3 carrots, cut in 3″ pieces
3–4 lb. lean corned beef brisket
2–3 medium onions, quartered
cabbage cut into small wedges
1–2 cups water

Recipe from: Pat Ciochetti

*Can be cooked in a 300-degree oven for 3 to 4 hours before adding vegetables.

Cal	Prot	Fat	Carb	Fiber	Chol	Sodium
320kc	22g	21g	12g	4g	75mg	200mg

GROUND BEEF ENTREES

Beef-Bean Casserole

1½ pounds ground beef
½ cup catsup
½ teaspoon mustard
1 tablespoons vinegar
dash Worcestershire sauce
3 tablespoons brown sugar
1 onion
1 can red kidney beans
1 can pork & beans
½ teaspoon salt
8 slices bacon

Brown meat in skillet; mix with other ingredients. put bacon on top. Bake 45–60 min.

Yield: 8 servings

Recipe from: Judy Morris

Cal	Prot	Fat	Carb	Fiber	Chol	Sodium
500kc	30g	28g	32g	7g	90mg	940mg

Beef-Bean Casserole (Revised)

Preheat oven to 350 degrees; spray a 10 or a 3 quart casserole and a nonstick skillet with vegetable spray. Brown ground sirloin in skillet; while meat is browning, combine remaining ingredients except bacon. When meat is cooked, add to bean mixture and mix well. Spoon mixture into a prepared casserole, lay bacon on top. Bake in 350 degree oven, uncovered, for 45–60 min.

Yield: 8 servings

vegetable spray
1 lb. ground beef sirloin
½ cup catsup
½ teaspoon yellow mustard
1 tablespoon white wine
   vinegar
dash Worcestershire sauce
2 tablespoons brown sugar
1 cup chopped onion
1 (16 oz.) can red kidney
   beans, drained
1 (16 oz.) can vegetarian
   baked beans
4 slices reduced-fat bacon, cut
   into 1" pieces

Cal	Prot	Fat	Carb	Fiber	Chol	Sodium
240kc	19g	4.5g	34g	9g	35mg	540mg

Ground Beef-Corn Casserole

1 lb. hamburger
2 tablespoons shortening
¼ cup chopped onion
2 eggs
¼ cup milk
1½ teaspoons salt
1½ cups bread crumbs
1 can cream style corn
2 teaspoons mustard
½ teaspoon thyme
¼ teaspoon oregano
2 tablespoons butter

Brown hamburger and onion in shortening. Add seasonings, eggs, milk, 1 cup crumbs, corn and mustard. Mix well and put into greased 2 quart casserole. Mix remaining crumbs and butter and sprinkle over top of casserole. Bake at 350 for 30–40 minutes.

Cal	Prot	Fat	Carb	Fiber	Chol	Sodium
340kc	19g	18g	26g	2g	95mg	920mg

Ground Beef-Corn Casserole (Revised)

Spray a 2 quart casserole and a non-stick skillet with vegetable spray; preheat oven to 350 degrees. Cook ground meat in skillet until almost done, add onion, cook until meat is browned and onions are tender. Add eggs, milk, corn, mustard, 1 cup crumbs, salt, thyme oregano; mix well, spoon into prepared casserole. Sprinkle remaining crumbs over meat mixture, carefully spray crumbs with vegetable spray for about 2 seconds. Bake in 350 degree oven for 30–40 minutes.

Yield: 8 servings

vegetable spray
1 lb. ground beef round or sirloin
¼ cup chopped onion
1 egg + 1 egg white
¼ cup reduced-fat milk
1 (14 ¾ oz.) can cream style corn
2 teaspoons yellow mustard
1½ cups bread crumbs
¼ teaspoon salt
½ teaspoon thyme
¼ teaspoon oregano

Cal	Prot	Fat	Carb	Fiber	Chol	Sodium
200kc	16g	4.5g	25g	1g	55mg	460mg

Beef

Meatball Strogonoff (sic)

Meatballs:
2 slices bread-broken up
2 lb. hamburger
1 onion-chopped fine
1 tsp. salt
¼ tsp. pepper
milk to moisten

Mix together to form balls. Brown in hot skillet. Add: 1 can mushrooms & juice, stir & brown with meatballs 1 can mushroom soup & 1 can beef broth, stir. Cook ½–¾ hour. Add: 1 cup sour cream, mix well and heat.

Serve over hot cooked noodles.

Cal	Prot	Fat	Carb	Fiber	Chol	Sodium
250kc	19g	20g	6g	<1g	66mg	669mg

Meatball Stroganoff (Revised)

In a large mixing bowl or food processor, combine sirloin, bread crumbs, onion, salt, oregano, thyme and black pepper, and just enough milk to help the meat balls stick together; shape into balls. Heat half the oil in a large skillet, add meat balls and brown, turning frequently to keep meatball's round shape, adding more oil if needed. While meatballs are browning; spray a 10 oven-safe baking dish with vegetable spray. When meatballs are brown, transfer to prepared baking dish. Brown mushrooms in pan drippings, add to meatballs. In a small bowl combine soup and broth, add to meatballs, stir. Cook ½–¾ hour over low heat or in 350 degree oven. Remove from heat; add sour cream blending well, heat slightly then serve immediately.

Serve over hot cooked noodles, rice or mashed potatoes.

Yield: 4 servings

1 lb. ground beef sirloin or
    ground turkey
½ cup course bread crumbs
1 small onion, chopped
¼ teaspoon salt
½ teaspoon oregano
⅛ teaspoon ground thyme
black pepper as desired
2 teaspoons oil, divided
3 tablespoons reduced-fat
    milk, (enough to moisten)
vegetable spray
1 cup sliced fresh mushrooms
1 (10 ¾ oz.) can low-fat,
    low-sodium condensed
    cream of mushroom soup
1 (17 oz.) can low-fat,
    low-sodium beef broth
1 cup fat-free or reduced-fat
    sour cream

Cal	Prot	Fat	Carb	Fiber	Chol	Sodium
380kc	28g	14g	30g	1g	105mg	790mg

Lasagna

Sauce:

1 lb. ground beef or ground
  turkey
1 large onion chopped
1 T. Italian seasoning
12 oz. can tomato paste
1 t. Tabasco sauce
¼ c. Worcestershire sauce
1 t garlic powder
⅓ c. sugar
pepper to taste
1½ tsp salt

Filling:

cottage cheese (drained)
mozzarella cheese
Parmesan cheese
lasagna noodles:

Brown meat and onion; season with Italian seasoning and garlic powder. Add 3 cups of water and the rest of the ingredients. Bring to a boil and then simmer 2 hours.

Cook 14–16 noodles according to package directions. Rinse each noodle with cold water (gently).

Mix drained cottage cheese & mozzarella cheese.

Butter lasagna pan then layer:
⅓ sauce
noodles
½ cheeses
noodles
⅓ sauce
noodles
½ cheeses
noodles
⅓ sauce
generously cover with Parmesan cheese

Cover with aluminum foil. Freeze at least 24 hours. Set out 2 hours before baking. Bake at 350 degrees for 1½ hours. Cool 15 minutes before serving.

Recipe from: Janet Shriver Farineau

Cal	Prot	Fat	Carb	Fiber	Chol	Sodium
370kc	24g	12g	41g	3g	45mg	900mg

Lasagna (Revised)

1 lb. ground turkey

1 cup chopped onion

3 cloves garlic, minced

½ teaspoon salt

¼ teaspoon crushed red pepper

1 tablespoon dried parsley flakes

1 tablespoon Italian seasoning

freshly ground black pepper to
taste

1 (12 oz.) can tomato paste

1 (4.5 oz.) tube Italian tomato
paste

3 cups water

¼ cup Worcestershire sauce

1 teaspoon Tabasco sauce

⅓ cup sugar

1 (16 oz.) box lasagna noodles

1 (16 oz.) container fat-free
cottage cheese

8 oz. mozzarella cheese, divided

½ cup Parmesan cheese

vegetable spray

Brown turkey, onion and garlic in large sauce pan. Add salt, crushed red pepper, parsley, Italian seasoning, and pepper, stir. Add both tomato paste, water, Worcestershire and Tabasco sauce and sugar. Bring to a boil, reduce heat and simmer for 2 hours.

Cook lasagna noodles according to package directions, drain, gently rinse with cold water, drain thoroughly, and set aside.

In a medium bowl combine cottage cheese, 4 oz. mozzarella cheese and ¼ cup Parmesan cheese, set aside.

Spray lasagna pan, approximately 9 × 16 , with vegetable spray. Layer in this order: ⅓ sauce, ¼ noodles, ½ cheeses, ¼ noodles, ⅓ sauce, ¼ noodles, ½ cheeses, remaining noodles, remaining sauce. Top with remaining 4 ounces of Mozzarella cheese, then sprinkle remaining ¼ cup Parmesan cheese over all. Cover with foil and freeze for at least 24 hours. Set out to thaw at least 3 hours before baking. Bake at 350 degrees for 1 hour, remove foil and continue to cook for 30 minutes or until browned. Cool 15 minutes before serving.

Yield: 12 servings

Cal	Prot	Fat	Carb	Fiber	Chol	Sodium
340kc	23g	8g	44g	3g	45mg	820mg

Mom's Meat Loaf

John's family loved this basic meat loaf.

1½ lb. lean ground beef
1 cup Wheaties cereal
½ cup milk
½ onion, finely chopped
1 tsp. green onion, finely chopped
1 tsp. salt
2 eggs

Mix everything together. Bake 1½ hours at 350 degrees.

Recipe from: Eleanor Shriver

Cal	Prot	Fat	Carb	Fiber	Chol	Sodium
320kc	24g	21g	6g	<1g	140mg	530mg

Mom's Meat Loaf (Revised)

Our family preferred a little more flavor and color to our meatloaf, so I made a few changes to Mom Shriver's basic recipe.

Preheat oven to 350 degrees, spray loaf pan with vegetable spray. In a large bowl or food processor combine ground beef, cereal, milk, onion, green pepper, salt, sage, and eggs; spoon into prepared pan. In a small bowl combine catsup, brown sugar, nutmeg, and dry mustard, spoon over meat loaf. Bake in 350 degree oven for 1½ hours.

Yield: 6 servings

*Can use ground turkey

vegetable spray
1½ lb. ground beef sirloin*
1 cup Wheaties or Corn Flakes cereal
½ cup reduced-fat milk
½ onion, finely chopped
¼ cup chopped green pepper
½ teaspoon salt
1 teaspoon sage
1 egg + 1 egg white
¼ cup catsup
3 tablespoons brown sugar
¼ teaspoon nutmeg
1 teaspoon dry mustard

Cal	Prot	Fat	Carb	Fiber	Chol	Sodium
220kc	25g	6g	16g	<1g	90mg	450mg

Beef

Peg's Dinner In One

½ lb. loose sausage or ground
    meat (beef) fried
½ cup uncooked rice put on
    and cook, cook first.
½ head cabbage sliced
1 can tomato soup or thin
    white sauce

Put alternately in cassorole (sic) & bake ½ hr.

Cal	Prot	Fat	Carb	Fiber	Chol	Sodium
350kc	20g	13g	39g	4g	55mg	560mg

Peg's Dinner In One (Revised)

Slice cabbage and onion*; brown sirloin in a non-stick skillet.

Preheat oven to 350 degrees; spray a 8 casserole with vegetable spray.

Place a layer of cabbage in casserole. Next, add browned meat and rice; then top with remaining cabbage. Combine flour and milk in a jar with lid; shake vigorously until smooth; pour into saucepan over medium-high heat. Stir constantly until mixture starts to thicken; add margarine, Worcestershire sauce, salt, and pepper. Spoon over top of casserole, sprinkle with paprika. Bake in 350 degree oven ½ hour.

Yield: 4 servings

*This is a great job for the food processor.

½ head small cabbage
1 small onion sliced
½ lb. ground beef sirloin
1 cup cooked white rice
¼ cup all-purpose flour
2 cups reduced-fat milk
1 tablespoon margarine
1 teaspoon
    Worcestershire sauce
½ teaspoon salt
black pepper to taste
paprika

Cal	Prot	Fat	Carb	Fiber	Chol	Sodium
270kc	19g	7g	34g	4g	35mg	460mg

John Marzette-Spegette (sic)

1 lb. ground beef
1 lb. ground pork
1 stalk celery
1 green pepper
1 can mushrooms
1 onion
1 qt. tomatoes
2 cans tomato soup
1 can water
1 lb. noodles (cooked & drained)
¼ lb. sharp cheese
Seasoning

Make meat into small balls, brown. Add remaining ingredients except noodles and cheese; bake 3 hours in slow oven. Cook noodles add to sauce; sprinkle cheese on top and bake ½ hour.

Recipe from: Isabelle Shriver Smail

Cal	Prot	Fat	Carb	Fiber	Chol	Sodium
660kc	35g	29g	66g	5g	95mg	690mg

Beef

John Marzette Spaghetti (Revised)

1 lb. ground beef sirloin
½ lb. turkey Italian sausage
2 ribs celery, chopped
½ green pepper, chopped
1 small onion, chopped
2 cloves garlic
1 cup fresh mushrooms, sliced
1 quart canned tomatoes
2 (10 ¾ oz.) cans low-fat,
    low-sodium condensed
    tomato soup
1 soup can water
2 teaspoons Italian seasoning
1 tablespoon Worcestershire
    sauce
½ teaspoon salt
1 bay leaf
1 lb. pasta of choice
½ lb. shredded, reduced-fat
    mozzarella or sharp
    cheddar cheese

Combine ground sirloin and sausage, shape into balls. Spray a 9×13 casserole and a large nonstick skillet. Add meat balls a few at a time to the hot skillet; brown, turning frequently until brown. Place meatballs in prepared 9×13 casserole.

While meatballs are browning; preheat oven to 350 degree. Sauté celery, pepper, onion and garlic in skillet drippings. When golden, add mushrooms; continue to cook about 2 minutes. Add tomatoes, soup, water, Italian seasoning, Worcestershire sauce, salt and bay leaf, bring to a boil; pour over meatballs. Cover, place in 350 degree oven and bake 2 hours, remove bay leaf and discard. About 15 minutes before time is complete; cook pasta according to manufacturer's directions. Add pasta to sauce and meatballs; sprinkle shredded cheese over top. Return to oven, uncovered, and continue to bake about 15–20 minutes or until cheese is melted and bubbly.

Yield: 34 meat balls-8 servings

Cal	Prot	Fat	Carb	Fiber	Chol	Sodium
300kc	26g	12g	20g	3g	55mg	1030mg

When I think back to the times when I had large vegetable gardens, it seemed that no matter how I tried to stagger planting my cabbage plants, they all would ripen about the same time. Therefore, I was always searching for a variety of ways to prepare cabbage. While living in the Pittsburgh area, I was talking to a friend from church one day, lamenting on the burden of too much cabbage, when she told me about a favorite of her family, "pigs-in-a-blanket." It was love at first taste, and became a favorite for my family. I would make these "pigs-in-a-blanket" by the dozen and freeze them when I was overloaded with cabbage. It was a lot of work, but the results were well worth it for the wonderful meals they provided during the long cold winter.

Pigs-in-a-Blanket

1 medium head cabbage
28 oz. tomato juice
2 pounds ground hamburger
2 eggs
3 cloves garlic, minced
⅓ cup rice, uncooked
½ tsp. salt
½ tsp. pepper
½ tsp. paprika
¼ cup sugar
28 oz. sauerkraut
1 large onion, chopped
1 tsp. garlic powder

Cut around core of cabbage, remove core; place cabbage in boiling water to cover, boil about 3–4 minutes. Drain and cool, when cool carefully remove 1 leaf at a time and set aside. Mix ground hamburger, rice, eggs and seasonings. Place 2–3 tablespoons of meat mixture on each leaf and roll leaf around meat. Layer ingredients in a large casserole or roasting pan, in this order: A layer of sauerkraut, sprinkle half the onions and garlic, then cabbage rolls. Cover rolls with remaining sauerkraut, onion and garlic. Pour tomato juice over all. Cover; bake 2 to 2½ hours at 325 degree.

Recipe from: Mary Thorpe

Cal	Prot	Fat	Carb	Fiber	Chol	Sodium
330kc	21g	17g	24g	6g	100mg	1016mg

Beef

Pigs-in-a-Blanket (Revised)

1 medium head cabbage
vegetable spray
2 lb. ground beef, sirloin or round
⅓ cup rice, uncooked
1 egg
½ teaspoon salt
freshly ground black pepper to
    taste
½ teaspoon paprika
1 teaspoon garlic powder
1 (28 oz.) jar sauerkraut
1 large onion, chopped
3 cloves garlic, minced
¼ cup sugar
1 (28 oz.) can tomato juice

Cut around core of cabbage, remove core; place cabbage in boiling water to cover, boil about 3–4 minutes. Drain and cool; carefully remove 1 leaf at a time placing on paper towel, set aside.

Preheat oven to 325 degrees; spray a large 9×13 baking dish or roasting pan with vegetable spray.

In a large mixing bowl combine ground beef, rice, egg and seasonings. Place 2–3 tablespoons of meat mixture on each leaf. (Remember the rice has not cooked, so the rice will expand as it cooks.) Gently tuck leaf around meat and secure with a wooden pick.* Repeat until all the filling has been used. Layer in this order in prepared baking dish: ½ sauerkraut, sprinkle half the onions and garlic, then cabbage rolls. Cover rolls with remaining sauerkraut, onion and garlic. Sprinkle sugar over all; pour tomato juice over all. Cover; bake at 325 degrees for 2 to 2½ hours.

Yield: 10 servings

*Cabbage rolls freeze beautifully, when ready to
cook, layer with other ingredients as directed above.

Cal	Prot	Fat	Carb	Fiber	Chol	Sodium
217kc	21g	5g	24g	5g	66mg	1045mg

Runzas

My friend Sue Brandt, who grew up in Nebraska, shared this recipe from her childhood. I was not familiar with runzas, but once I made them, I'll never forget them. I have several friends and neighbors from that region, and when asked about runzas they all exclaimed that runzas were their favorite comfort foods.

Dough:

2 cups warm water

2 pkg. yeast

½ cup sugar

1½ teaspoons salt

1 egg

¼ cup margarine, melted, cooled

6½ cups flour

Filling:

1½ lb. ground hamburger

½ cup chopped onion

3 cups cabbage, shredded

½ cup water

1½ tsp. salt

½ tsp. pepper

dash Tabasco

Dough: Beat together water, yeast, sugar, salt, egg, margarine and 3 cups flour. Stir in remaining flour. Let rise in refrigerator 4 hours or at room temperature 1 hour.

Filling: Brown hamburger and onion, (do not drain fat) add remaining ingredients. Cover and simmer 15–20 minutes. Let cool. Roll dough into rectangle and cut into 16 squares. Place 2 tablespoons filling on each square. Fold corners to center and seal edges. Bake at 350 degrees until golden brown.

Recipe from: Susan Sidell Brandt

Cal	Prot	Fat	Carb	Fiber	Chol	Sodium
350kc	14g	11g	47g	2g	40mg	510mg

Runzas (Revised)

Eat these like a hamburger, serving with dill pickle and maybe french fries.

Filling:
1 lb. ground beef sirloin
1 medium onion, chopped
8 cups cabbage, shredded
⅓ cup water
1 teaspoon salt
1 teaspoon black pepper
dash Tabasco

Dough:*
2 cups warm water, 120 degrees
2 pkg. yeast
½ cup sugar
1 teaspoon salt
1 egg
¼ cup margarine, melted, cooled
6½ to 7 cups all-purpose flour

Filling: Brown ground meat and onion in a large kettle; add cabbage and water. Cover and simmer about 30 minutes or until cabbage is tender. Remove lid and simmer until all liquid is gone. Refrigerate to chill thoroughly.

Dough: Beat together water, yeast, sugar, salt, egg, margarine and 3 cups flour. Stir in remaining flour. Turn dough out on a lightly floured surface; knead about 2 minutes. Place in large greased bowl, turn once to grease dough; cover with wax paper then a dish towel. Let rise in refrigerator 4 hours or at room temperature 1 hour, or until doubled in bulk.

Divide dough into 4 sections. Working with one section, divide into 4 balls, roll dough into circles, trying to make thinner at outer edges. Place ¼ cup filling on each circle. Fold opposite sides together; pinch edges to seal. Place seam side down on cookie sheet. **Cover with cloth and let rise for 30 minutes or until puffy. Bake in a 350 degrees oven about 35 minutes or until golden brown. ***

Yield: 16 runzas

*You can use frozen bread dough; thaw before using.
**You can cover the runzas with plastic wrap at this point and refrigerate for up to five hours before allowing to rise and then baking.
***After baking, they freeze well and can be reheated in oven or microwave.

Cal	Prot	Fat	Carb	Fiber	Chol	Sodium
300kc	13g	5g	52g	3g	25mg	360mg

Porcupine Meat Balls

This is a great budget stretcher; you could always rely on inexpensive ground hamburger and rice for a variety of meals as payday was approaching.

1 pound hamburger
¼ cup uncooked rice
¼ cup chopped onion
1 egg
1 teaspoon salt
1 can tomato soup

Shape into balls. Brown in 2 tablespoons shortening with small garlic clove minced. Cover with the rest of soup and 1 cup of water. Cover pan. Simmer 40 minutes or until rice is tender. Serves 6

Cal	Prot	Fat	Carb	Fiber	Chol	Sodium
260kc	17g	15g	14g	g0	m85g	m730g

Porcupine Meat Balls (Revised)

Spray a 10 baking dish with vegetable spray. In a medium bowl combine sirloin, rice, onion, garlic, egg, salt, and oregano; shape into balls (about 16). Heat 1 teaspoon oil in a nonstick skillet, add meat balls; using two forks, turn balls frequently until browned; place in prepared baking dish. Repeat with oil and meat balls until all meat balls are browned. Blend soup and water; pour over meat balls. Cover, bake in 350 degree oven for 40 minutes.

Yield: 6 servings

We like this served over mashed potatoes or noodles and with a green salad.

vegetable spray
1 lb. ground beef sirloin, or ground turkey
¼ cup uncooked rice
¼ cup chopped onion
1 clove garlic, minced
1 egg
¼ teaspoon salt
½ teaspoon oregano
2 teaspoons oil divided
1 (10 ¾ oz.) can low-fat, low-sodium condensed tomato soup
1 soup can water

Cal	Prot	Fat	Carb	Fiber	Chol	Sodium
180kc	17g	6g	15g	<1g	70mg	340mg

Beef Stuffed Peppers

4 medium green peppers
1 tblsp. margarine
½ lb. lean ground beef
½ cup chopped onion
¼ tsp. salt
dash pepper
1 tsp. Worcestershire sauce
¾ cup cooked rice
1 can tomato soup, condensed

Remove tops & seeds from peppers; submerge in boiling water and cook 5 minutes; drain. Brown beef & onions in margarine; stir in ½ can soup and remaining ingredients. Spoon meat mixture into peppers, place upright in a pan. Spoon remaining soup over peppers, bake at 375 degrees for 30 minutes. Freeze before baking if desired.

Recipe from: Mary Thorpe

Cal	Prot	Fat	Carb	Fiber	Chol	Sodium
295kc	14g	14g	30g	3g	39mg	657mg

Beef Stuffed Peppers (Revised)

Remove tops and seeds from peppers; submerge in boiling water and cook 5 minutes; drain on a paper towel. Spray a 5×7 loaf pan with vegetable spray; preheat oven to 350 degrees. Heat oil in a non-stick skillet; add beef and onions, cook until brown. Add ½ can soup and remaining ingredients; stir well. Spoon meat mixture into peppers, place upright in prepared pan. Spoon remaining soup over peppers. Bake in a 350-degree oven for 30 minutes.

Yield: 4 servings

These freeze beautifully. To freeze: Stuff peppers as above, stand upright in a container with sides; cover and freeze. When frozen firm, place stuffed peppers in a zip-lock plastic bag. When ready to cook proceed as directed above.

vegetable spray
4 medium green peppers
1 teaspoon olive oil
½ lb. ground beef sirloin or ground turkey
½ cup chopped onion
1 (10 ¾oz) can low-fat, low-sodium, condensed tomato soup
¼ teaspoon salt
freshly ground black pepper
1 teaspoon Worcestershire sauce
¾ cup cooked rice

Cal	Prot	Fat	Carb	Fiber	Chol	Sodium
218kc	14g	5g	31g	3g	30mg	475mg

Fish

Fish

Few things recall such precious memories as thinking about my dad, Aud Day, and his love for fishing, oh how my dad loved to fish. I think he would rather fish than eat what he caught. This is really saying something, because he certainly loved to eat Mom's fried fish.

I have wonderful memories of growing up in the beautiful northeastern hills of Tennessee, surrounded by our large and happy family. We lived among the sparkling lakes of the Tennessee Valley Authority and spent a great deal of our recreational time on one lake or another. I never felt neglected because of my dad's hobby of fishing, he would just take one of my siblings or me fishing with him. Not only did my family love to fish and eat, but also we were happy just to be on the lake in Dad's old boat with the outboard motor. We would cruise the lake, exploring little coves, and eventually Dad would slip into a peaceful cove where we would swim, sunbathe or maybe water ski. As we tired of the sun, wind, and spray, Dad would anchor the boat, and we would partake of a wonderful picnic supper. It could be fried chicken and potato salad, or maybe we would build up a fire and have grilled hot dogs and hamburgers. At other times, on special occasions, Dad would clean a "mess" of fish and Mom would fry them on the spot. It didn't matter where she fried them; Mom's fried fish was always a crispy golden brown on the outside and moist on the inside.

Mom never used a recipe, she just cooked with a dab of this and a shake of that, and since all of us children had to help in the kitchen, we learned to cook Mom's way. I remember Mom and Dad having fish fries for family and friends, where they provided the fish and others brought the side dishes. These happy get-togethers continued until my parents were elderly. As Mom began to age, she would fry fish until she got hot and tired then would hand the job over to one of us. The temperature of the oil had to be just so hot and the fish had to be just so brown. Mom was never far away, just in case we needed her guidance.

Even if I can't give you my mom's recipe for fried fish, I can share her method and the ingredients she used. I think I have captured a portion of her art of preparing delicious fried fish, I hope you enjoy it.

Mom's Fried Fish

1 lb. fresh pan fish fillets, e.g.,
   bass, catfish, or any mild fish
1 egg, beaten
1 tablespoon milk or water
½ cup or more yellow cornmeal
¼ teaspoon salt
black pepper to taste
dash paprika
¼ cup vegetable oil

Rinse fish and pat dry, cut into individual serving pieces. In a small bowl, beat egg with milk or water, set aside. Mom always used an old pie pan to combine cornmeal, salt, pepper and paprika. She would dip the fish, one piece at a time, in the egg, then into the cornmeal mixture, then she would start her gentle circular shaking motion to coat fish. It was a treat to just watch her do this. (I must remember to tell you how she mashed potatoes.) Heat oil in a large heavy iron or electric skillet; when hot, carefully add fish. Fry on medium-high until brown on both sides.

Yield: 3–4 servings, or if you really love it 2–3 servings.

Serve with mashed potatoes, coleslaw and corn bread.

Cal	Prot	Fat	Carb	Fiber	Chol	Sodium
310kc	22g	18g	14g	1g	115mg	210mg

Oven Fried Fish (Revised)

John and I eat fish a couple of times a week and while nothing can compare to Mom's fried fish, I do think there are good alternatives we can use for the sake of our health.

Following are two recipes I think you will enjoy.

Preheat oven to 450 degrees; spray broiler pan and rack with vegetable spray.

Place flour on a paper towel. Combine egg white, hot sauce and sour cream in a shallow dish, beat with a fork until frothy. Combine cornmeal, seasoned salt and pepper on another paper towel. Rinse fish, cut into serving size pieces. Dredge each piece in flour, dip in egg white mixture, then cornmeal. Place fish on prepared broiler pan. Carefully spray breaded fish with vegetable spray for about two seconds. Bake in 450 degree oven for 12–15 minutes or until fish is golden brown and flakes easily when tested with a fork.

vegetable spray
½ cup all-purpose flour
1 egg white
1 teaspoon hot sauce, as desired
½ cup fat-free sour cream
1 cup corn meal
½ teaspoon seasoned salt
black pepper
1 lb. fresh pan fish fillets, e.g.,
   bass, catfish, orange roughy

Yield: 4 servings

Cal	Prot	Fat	Carb	Fiber	Chol	Sodium
330kc	25g	4g	44g	3g	70mg	320mg

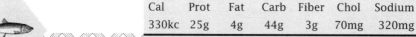

Fish

Breaded Baked Fish

vegetable spray
1 lb. fresh mild white fish fillets,
    i.e., orange roughy, scrod or
    cod
2 cups course bread crumbs
¼ cup grated Parmesan cheese
1 egg white +1 tablespoon water
1 tablespoon parsley
dash of lemon pepper
dash garlic powder

Preheat oven to 400 degrees; spray broiler pan and rack with vegetable spray. Rinse fish and pat dry. Combine bread crumbs and cheese on a piece of waxed paper. In shallow bowl combine egg whites with water; beat with fork until frothy. Dip fish into egg white then dredge in crumbs to coat well; place on prepared broiler pan, sprinkle with parsley, lemon pepper and garlic powder. Carefully spray breaded fish with vegetable spray for about 2 seconds. Bake in a 400 degree oven about 15–20 minutes or until fish flakes when tested with a fork.

To microwave: Prepare fish as above. Place fish in a microwave-safe baking dish with thickest portion of fish on the outside of dish; cover with waxed paper. Microwave about 2½ to 3 minutes on high or until fish flakes when tested with a fork.

Yield: 4 servings

Cal	Prot	Fat	Carb	Fiber	Chol	Sodium
330kc	27g	6g	40g	1g	30mg	670mg

Vegetables

Vegetables

At the first hint of spring, my thoughts go to gardening. I have always loved gardening and the nearness to God I feel as I watch daily for the tiny seeds to break through the soil. Once planted, I continue with watchful eyes as the seedlings grow, stretching their tips to the sun, developing into mature plants, and later producing babies of their own. My favorite garden was in McMurray, Pennsylvania, where I had an exceptionally prolific vegetable garden. This garden produced in a manner similar to the Garden of Eden—I planted, they grew. I will admit I always planted extra for the deer, raccoons, and ground hogs, who usually obliged me by leaving more than enough for my family and friends.

It seems to me there are certain crops that produce until you want to shout "uncle"; tomatoes, zucchini, and green peppers are just a few I can think of. After these crops start producing and you are harvesting every day, then comes the canning, freezing, and sharing with others. You eventually fear you will run out of friends, neighbors, and family members to give them to. I've even been tempted to leave some to share with the trash collectors.

Happily, we had lots of family and a wealth of friends to share our harvest with, and they in turn shared their favorite recipes with us. We especially enjoyed the recipes from friends of different ethnic backgrounds, of which there were many in the Pittsburgh area. I had great fun collecting and experimenting with these great recipes.

Baked Beans

1 jar (3lb) Great Northern
   beans
1 cup light brown sugar, firmly
   packed
¼ lb. bacon, cut into small
   pieces
1 tsp. Worcestershire sauce
1 onion, chopped fine
1 tblsp. molasses
1 tsp dry mustard
¾ of a small bottle of catsup

Mix all ingredients together, put in pan or casserole. Bake at 350 degrees for about 2 hours.

Recipe from: Caroline Shriver

Cal	Prot	Fat	Carb	Fiber	Chol	Sodium
336kc	14g	6g	58g	7g	9mg	420mg

Baked Beans (Revised)

Preheat oven to 350 degrees; spray a 9″ casserole with vegetable spray.

Combine all ingredients except bacon; spoon into prepared casserole, place bacon on top. Cover; bake in 350 degree oven for about 2 hours.

Yield: 10 servings

vegetable spray
3-(15 oz.) cans Great Northern
   beans
1 cup light brown sugar, firmly
   packed
1 teaspoon Worcestershire
   sauce
1 onion, chopped fine
1 tablespoon molasses
1 teaspoon dry mustard
¾ cup catsup
4 slices reduced- fat bacon,
   cut into small pieces

Cal	Prot	Fat	Carb	Fiber	Chol	Sodium
275kc	11g	2g	56g	7g	2mg	279mg

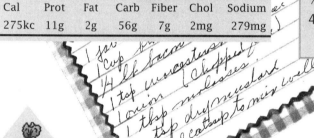

Vegetables

Cut (Schnitzel) Beans

2 lbs. green beans, cut into
  bite size pieces
3 tablespoons bacon drippings
1 large onion, chopped
1 teaspoon salt
2 large tomatoes, chopped

Cook beans and onions in enough water to cover, add salt and bacon drippings. Cook until done, add tomatoes cook about an hour longer. Add more water as needed.

Cal	Prot	Fat	Carb	Fiber	Chol	Sodium
100kc	2g	5g	11g	5g	5mg	320mg

Green Beans & Stewed Tomatoes (Revised)

Cook beans, onion, garlic, oil and salt in just enough water to cover, for about 45 minutes. Add tomatoes and sugar, continue to cook for about 30 minutes or until beans are tender.

Yield: 8 servings

*Can substitute canned beans and tomatoes.

2 lbs. fresh cut green beans
½ small onion, chopped
1 clove garlic, minced
2 teaspoons vegetable oil
½ teaspoon salt, or to taste
2 medium tomatoes, chopped
1 tablespoon sugar

Cal	Prot	Fat	Carb	Fiber	Chol	Sodium
60kc	2g	1g	11g	5g	0mg	150mg

Green Beans & Potatoes

This dish was a staple with my family while I was growing up. My dad always had a garden and the whole family loved the way Mom would prepare his fresh green beans. She would serve them with coleslaw and corn bread. Yum, yum!

mess of fresh green beans
fat-back (salt pork) or ham hock
salt
little new red potatoes

Cal	Prot	Fat	Carb	Fiber	Chol	Sodium
255kc	4g	12g	17g	5g	13mg	520mg

Green Beans & Potatoes (Revised)

Thoroughly wash beans, remove ends and break into 1″ lengths. Place beans, bacon and enough water to cover in a medium saucepan. Bring to a boil, reduce heat and continue to cook about 1 hour. Using a slotted spoon carefully lift a scoop of beans and place potatoes underneath. Continue to cook approximately 20 minutes or until beans and potatoes are tender. Add salt before serving.

2 lb. fresh green beans
¼ lb. Canadian bacon, or
   reduced- fat bacon, diced
1 lb. small red potatoes
1 teaspoon salt

Yield: 8 servings

Cal	Prot	Fat	Carb	Fiber	Chol	Sodium
90kc	4g	.5g	17g	5g	5mg	450mg

Vegetables

Vegetables

ur daughter-in-law, Angie, remembers that her great-aunt Pauline used to always bring a baked cabbage dish to family reunions.

Baked Cabbage

6 slices bread
milk to cover
3 eggs
1 onion
½ head cabbage
½ cup grated cheese
salt and pepper

Chop cabbage, soak bread in the milk; beat eggs mix all together except cheese, top with cheese. Bake 350 for about 30 minutes or until tender.

Cal	Prot	Fat	Carb	Fiber	Chol	Sodium
170kc	9g	7g	20g	4g	105mg	250mg

Baked Cabbage (Revised)

Preheat oven to 350 degrees; spray a 9×9 baking dish with vegetable spray.

In a large mixing bowl, soak bread in the milk for 5 minutes; add eggs, salt, peppers, onion and cabbage, stir. Spoon mixture in prepared baking dish; top with grated cheese. Bake at 350 degrees for 50 minutes.

Yield: 6 servings

vegetable spray
6 slices white bread, cubed
2 cups reduced-fat milk
1 egg, + 3 egg whites or ¾
    cup egg substitute, beaten
½ cup finely chopped onion
2 cups shredded cabbage
½ cup reduced fat Cheddar
    cheese
¼ teaspoon salt
dash red pepper
⅛ teaspoon black pepper

Cal	Prot	Fat	Carb	Fiber	Chol	Sodium
160kc	10g	4g	20g	2g	35mg	370mg

Fried Cabbage

1 medium head cabbage
¼ cup bacon drippings
½ cup minced onion
salt & pepper
¼ cup water

Cut cabbage into wedges, heat grease in iron skillet add cabbage, onions, salt, pepper, and water. Cook slow until everything is tender.

Recipe from: Oma Day

Cal	Prot	Fat	Carb	Fiber	Chol	Sodium
80kc	1g	6g	6g	6g	5mg	45mg

Fried Cabbage (Revised)

Cut cabbage into wedges, remove core. In large saucepan, heat oil; add onions, sauté until golden brown. Add cabbage, salt, pepper, and water. Cover; reduce heat to simmer, continue to cook 20 minutes or until cabbage is tender. Stir in margarine.

Yield: 10 servings

1 medium head cabbage
1 tablespoon vegetable oil
½ cup chopped onion
½ teaspoon salt
freshly ground black pepper to
    taste
¼ cup water
½ tablespoon margarine

Cal	Prot	Fat	Carb	Fiber	Chol	Sodium
45kc	1g	2g	6g	6g	0mg	140mg

Pennsylvania Dutch Cabbage

1 small to medium head
  of cabbage
1 egg
1 tablespoon sugar
dash pepper
1 teaspoon salt

Shred cabbage on medium cutter, place in saucepan, add salt. Cover pan and steam over low heat until very tender, about 20–30 minutes. In a small bowl beat the egg; add the sugar, salt, pepper and vinegar. When cabbage is tender, stir in egg mixture. Heat for 5 minutes. Serve immediately

Yield: 8 servings

Cal	Prot	Fat	Carb	Fiber	Chol	Sodium
45kc	2g	1g	8g	3g	25mg	320mg

Succotash

This was a traditional side dish for the Shrivers on Thanksgiving or Christmas.

Cook lima beans until almost tender; add corn, bring to a boil, reduce heat to simmer and simmer for about 10–15 minutes. Add margarine, salt, and pepper, stir.

1 (10 oz.) pkg. frozen lima
  beans
1 cup frozen corn*
2 teaspoons margarine
¼ teaspoon salt
black pepper to taste

Yield: 6 servings

*This is delicious when made with fresh corn kernels, cut off the cob.

Cal	Prot	Fat	Carb	Fiber	Chol	Sodium
80kc	4g	1.5g	15g	3g	0mg	130mg

Isabelle's Baked Corn

1 can whole kernel corn
1 can creamed corn
3 tablespoons margarine,
    melted
2 eggs, beaten
milk
bread crumbs

Put corn, eggs, most of margarine into casserole, pour milk over all, just enough to come up to the top of corn. Sprinkle bread crumbs over and drizzle with rest of margarine, bake 350 oven, 45 minutes, or until custard like.

Recipe from: Isabelle Shriver Smail

Cal	Prot	Fat	Carb	Fiber	Chol	Sodium
200kc	6g	8g	29g	2g	50mg	470mg

Isabelle's Baked Corn (Revised)

Spray 2–3 quart casserole with vegetable spray; preheat oven to 350 degrees.

In a large mixing bowl combine both cans corn, sugar, black pepper, eggs, pimento, sour cream, margarine and half and half, set aside. In a small bowl combine cornmeal, baking powder, flour, and salt; stir into corn mixture and pour into prepared casserole. Bake in a 350 degree oven, for one hour or until inserted knife comes out clean.

Yield: 8 servings

vegetable spray
1 (15 oz) can whole kernel corn
1 (15 oz) can creamed corn
1 teaspoon sugar
freshly ground black pepper
1 egg, +2 egg whites, beaten
2 tablespoons drained pimento
8 ounces reduced-fat sour cream
2 tablespoons margarine, melted
¼ cup fat-free half-and-half or more
½ cup cornmeal
2 teaspoons baking powder
2 tablespoons flour

Cal	Prot	Fat	Carb	Fiber	Chol	Sodium
180kc	7g	5g	30g	2g	25mg	630mg

Vegetables

Audrey's Corn Soup*

This was one of the Shriver family's favorite summertime dishes. But, alas, Mom Shriver just added a little of this and a lot of that and never wrote it down. Our daughter, Audrey, always loved Grandma Shrivers' corn soup and you could count on her being in the kitchen to help her Grandma prepare it. After Audrey married and moved away, she developed this recipe to share with those of us who could not remember how Mom made it.

8 ears fresh corn on cob
1 tablespoon butter or
    margarine
½–1 cup reduced-fat milk
    (depending on size of pan)
¼ teaspoon salt
dash freshly ground pepper
1 teaspoon sugar

Using a very sharp knife cut down each row of corn to slit each kernel, cut off very tops of kernels from cob, then using the side of knife, scrape the fleshy part of kernel to get all the juice and remaining corn kernel. Place in heavy saucepan, add milk just to come to the top of corn, add butter. Using low heat, bring to almost a simmer, but don't let it boil. (This will take 20–30 minutes). Stir frequently, add salt, pepper, & sugar. Cover & set aside until ready to serve.

Yield: 8 servings

Recipe from: Audrey Shriver Scalzo

*Don't be confused by the name, this is served as a side dish, not actually a soup.

Cal	Prot	Fat	Carb	Fiber	Chol	Sodium
180kc	6g	3g	37g	2g	0mg	125mg

Turnip Greens

a mess* of really fresh turnip
   greens
salt pork or ham hock
salt, pepper, sugar
hot chili sauce

Wash greens over and over in water, looking carefully for bugs. Put salt pork in large kettle with water; cook for about 1 hour. Add greens, cook until greens are tender about 30–40 minutes depending on how tender they are. Add seasonings.

Recipe from: Oma Day

*A "mess" is enough for one meal.

Cal	Prot	Fat	Carb	Fiber	Chol	Sodium
177kc	2.6g	12g	15g	<1g	13mg	545mg

Turnip Greens (Revised)

Place ham hock and onion in a large kettle and add water to cover. cook over medium heat cook about 1 hour. Thoroughly wash greens several times in cool water, drain. Remove hard center vein, and chop coarsely. Add to liquid in kettle, cover. Bring mixture to a boil, add remaining ingredients; reduce heat to low and cook 35–40 minutes or until greens are tender.

Yield: 4 servings

1 ham hock, trim as much
   fat off as possible
1 medium onion, chopped
1½ lbs. fresh turnip or
   mustard greens
1 teaspoon salt
black pepper as desired
2 tablespoons sugar
Louisiana hot sauce

Cal	Prot	Fat	Carb	Fiber	Chol	Sodium
122kc	7g	5g	15g	<1g	13mg	401mg

Vegetables

Sautéed Greens

1 lb. fresh collard, kale, chard,
turnip, mustard, broccoli
tops or any fresh greens
2 teaspoons olive oil
½–1 teaspoon balsamic
vinegar

I love to use most any kind of greens. I simply wash them thoroughly, drain, remove the tough center vein, and chop them. Heat olive oil in a wok. When hot, add greens and sauté until tender. Again, this depends on how tender the greens are when raw. Add balsamic vinegar and blend—so quick, easy, and nutritious. Yum, yum!

Cal	Prot	Fat	Carb	Fiber	Chol	Sodium
55kc	2g	3g	6g	1g	0mg	55mg

Fried Okra

Okra is one of those prolific garden crops I talked about earlier. It keeps bearing until everyone you know has had more than their fill. Thankfully, it is also a very versatile food and can be prepared many ways: stewed with tomatoes, in gumbo, or our very favorite way—fried.

Wash & cut okra in slices, roll around in cornmeal & salt. Fry in hot fat until brown and tender.

Recipe from: Oma Day

okra
about ½ cup bacon grease or
vegetable oil
little cornmeal
salt

Cal	Prot	Fat	Carb	Fiber	Chol	Sodium
300kc	3g	20g	19g	3g	30mg	500mg

Fried Okra (Revised)

1 lb. fresh okra*
vegetable spray
1 tablespoons olive oil
2 tablespoons cornmeal
½ teaspoon salt
dash cayenne pepper
dash paprika

Wash and drain okra; cut into ⅛–¼″ slices. Place in medium bowl, sprinkle cornmeal salt, pepper, and paprika over okra, toss gently. Spray a medium nonstick skillet with vegetable spray, add oil; when hot, add okra, cooking on medium heat about 5 minutes. Reduce heat to low; cover and steam about 4–5 minutes. Remove cover, increase heat to medium-high, cooking until brown and tender. Serve immediately.

Yield: 4 servings

*To test for fresh okra, snap off a bottom tip. If it snaps crisply, it's fresh, if it only bends, it is not fresh.

Cal	Prot	Fat	Carb	Fiber	Chol	Sodium
80kc	3g	3.5g	12g	3g	0mg	340mg

rowing up in the South, sweet potatoes were one of our favorite foods. Mom would prepare them the same as she would prepare white potatoes. You can bake them, mash them, french fry them, make them candied—let your imagination run wild. Here are some of the more popular ways to prepare sweet potatoes.

Baked Sweet Potatoes

Choose sweet potatoes of uniform size and similar shape, so the baking time will be the same. Scrub, pierce skin with a fork; place in shallow baking pan. Bake in a 450 degree oven until tender, about 45–50 minutes for a medium potato. Serve as you would a white potato with butter or reduced-fat margarine; salt and pepper as desired.

Microwaved Sweet Potatoes

Choose sweet potatoes of uniform size and similar shape, so the baking time will be the same. Scrub, pierce skin with a fork; place on a paper towel. Microwave on high 7–8 minutes, depending on how many you are cooking at the same time, cook until tender. Serve as you would a white potato with butter or reduced-fat margarine; salt and pepper as desired.

Mashed Sweet Potatoes

Prepare the same as for mashed potatoes, see page 143.
Chopped dates, raisins or chopped nuts may be added to mashed potatoes.
For a variation sprinkle top of potatoes with a little cloves or cinnamon.

Stuffed Sweet Potatoes

4 sweet potatoes
vegetable spray
1 tablespoon butter or reduced
    fat margarine
3–4 tablespoons warm fat-free
    half-and-half
1 tablespoon brown sugar
dash of cinnamon
dash of salt
½ cup coarse bread crumbs

Bake potatoes as above; cut lengthwise into halves. Using a spoon, gently scoop most of the pulp from the skin, being careful not to tear skin. Place pulp in a mixing bowl and mash with a potato masher.

Preheat oven to 375 degrees; spray baking dish with vegetable spray. To the pulp add butter, half-and-half, sugar, cinnamon and salt. Beat in with a fork to fluff potatoes. Carefully fill the shells and sprinkle tops with bread crumbs. Bake in 375 degree oven until heated through and crumbs are browned.

Yield: 4 servings

Cal	Prot	Fat	Carb	Fiber	Chol	Sodium
181kc	2g	3g	46g	2g	3mg	81mg

Candied Sweet Potatoes

Whether served with ham or turkey, this dish was always a part of our traditional Easter, Thanksgiving, and Christmas meals.

Scrub potatoes, cook until tender. Peel, cut in quarters, drizzle with butter, sprinkle with sugar and bake in 400 degree oven until brown and bubbly.

sweet potatoes or yams
brown sugar
salt
butter

Candied Sweet Potatoes (Revised)

4 medium sweet potatoes
½ cup brown sugar
1½ tablespoons margarine
⅓ cup pineapple or orange juice
dash nutmeg, cinnamon or cloves

Choose potatoes of uniform size, scrub thoroughly. Place in large pan, cover with boiling water, bring to a gentle boil, cook for 25 minutes or more until potatoes are tender when pierced with a fork. Drain, peel, and cut into quarters.

Preheat oven to 400 degrees: In a large range- and oven-safe dish, melt margarine over medium heat, sprinkle with sugar, stirring to blend well. Add juice and let simmer about 5 minutes. Add potatoes, sprinkle with nutmeg and salt; continue to cook for about 5 minutes, turn with 2 forks to coat potatoes with glaze. Bake, uncovered, in 400 degree oven for about 20–30 minutes.

Yield: 5 servings

Cal	Prot	Fat	Carb	Fiber	Chol	Sodium
240kc	2g	2.5g	53g	2g	0mg	55mg

We never followed a recipe for this dish, it was all by sight, feel, and taste. Everyone had their own way of preparing mashed potatoes, as well as a favorite method of mashing the potatoes; they would use a potato ricer, electric mixer, or a simple hand held potato masher. My mom used to make mashed potatoes quite often, so it all just came natural to her, the peeling, cooking, seasoning, and mashing. My mom always used the hand held potato masher; she would start with a slow movement, then work up to a fairly fast rhythm of beating. She had one unique trait in the way she moved her body as she mashed them. Along with the beating, she would swing her hips in the same rhythm with the beating—she could certainly get her hips moving to the beat. We used to have great fun watching Mom mash the potatoes and she would laugh right along with us.

Mashed Potatoes

6 medium potatoes
2 tablespoons + 1 teaspoon
   butter or margarine
¼ cup reduced-fat milk, warm
¼ teaspoon salt
black pepper if desired

Wash, peel and cut potatoes into small cubes; place in a medium pan, cover with water. Bring to a boil, reduce heat to low and simmer until tender, about 20 minutes. Drain; mash, using a potato masher or ricer. Add 2 tablespoons margarine and milk; beat with a large spoon until light and fluffy**; stir in salt to taste. Pile into serving dish, leaving surface fluffy, then top with remaining margarine and a dash of pepper.

Yield: 5 servings

*To reduce fat grams and calories; reduce margarine from 2 tablespoons to 1 tablespoon and substitute fat-free half-and-half or skim evaporated milk for regular milk.
**I don't like my mashed potatoes too smooth, I prefer to leave a few small lumps.

Cal	Prot	Fat	Carb	Fiber	Chol	Sodium
210kc	4g	6g	38g	4g	0mg	210mg

Yellow Squash Casserole

2 cups cooked, mashed yellow
    squash
3–4 teaspoons sugar
¼ cup onion, finely chopped
½ cup dry bread crumbs
2 eggs, beaten
salt & pepper
1 tablespoon butter
½ cup cheese, grated

Combine all except butter & cheese, place in 1½ quart greased baking dish. Dot with butter & sprinkle with cheese. Bake 350 degrees 30 minutes.

Cal	Prot	Fat	Carb	Fiber	Chol	Sodium
160kc	6g	7g	18g	2g	75mg	170mg

Yellow Squash Casserole (Revised)

Cook squash in a small amount of water about 30–35 minutes until very tender, drain and mash slightly. While squash is cooking, preheat oven to 350 degrees; spray a 1-quart baking dish with vegetable spray. Add sugar, onion, bread crumbs, eggs, salt, and pepper to squash, stir. Spoon into prepared baking dish. Drizzle with margarine and sprinkle with cheese. Bake in 350 degrees oven for 30 minutes.

Yield: 6 servings

3 cups yellow squash, diced
vegetable spray
3 teaspoons sugar
¼ cup onion, finely chopped
½ cup coarse, dry breadcrumbs
1 egg, + 2 egg whites or ½ cup
    egg substitute, beaten
1–2 tablespoons canned diced
    green chilies
¼ teaspoon salt
freshly ground black pepper to taste
2 teaspoons margarine

Cal	Prot	Fat	Carb	Fiber	Chol	Sodium
130kc	6g	3g	22g	3g	30mg	270mg

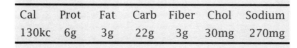

Sauces

Sauces

Meat Sauce

Good for basting pork roast, pork chops, ham, or ham loaf.

1 cup vinegar
1 cup water
2 cups brown sugar
4 tsp. mustard

Yield: 14 (¼ cup) servings

Cal	Prot	Fat	Carb	Fiber	Chol	Sodium
120kc	0g	0g	32g	0g	0mg	30mg

Tomato Sauce for Meat

Mix all ingredients together; simmer till thick. Makes ½ gal.

Yield: 16 (¼ cup) servings

(Quantities in parentheses are added by author.)

6 (6 oz.) cans tomato paste
1 (16 oz.) bottle catsup
½ pint (1 cup) pickle relish
¾ lb (2 cups + 2 tblsp) brown
    sugar
½ cup vinegar
5 small onions chopped
3 or 4 bay leaves
1 tsp. salt
1 tsp. celery salt
½ tsp. pepper

Cal	Prot	Fat	Carb	Fiber	Chol	Sodium
200kc	3g	.5g	50g	4g	0mg	1210mg

Vanilla Sauce

This is especially good on gingerbread, apple pudding page 173, or velvet crumb cake.

1 cup sugar
2 cups boiling water
2 tablespoons cornstarch
4 tablespoons butter
2 teaspoons vanilla
½ teaspoon salt

Combine sugar, cornstarch and salt, add water, bring to a boil. When thick, remove from heat; add butter and vanilla.

Cal	Prot	Fat	Carb	Fiber	Chol	Sodium
106kc	1g	4g	18g	0g	10mg	138mg

Vanilla Sauce (Revised)

Combine sugar, cornstarch, and salt in small saucepan, blend very thoroughly.

Place over medium-high heat, stirring constantly add boiling water; continue to stir until mixture thickens slightly. Remove from heat; add margarine and vanilla, stirring well.

Yield: 12 (¼ cup) servings

1 cup sugar
2 tablespoons cornstarch
dash salt
2 cups boiling water
1 tablespoon margarine
2 teaspoons vanilla

Cal	Prot	Fat	Carb	Fiber	Chol	Sodium
80kc	0g	.1g	18g	0g	0mg	14mg

Sauces

Brown Sugar Sauce

¾ cup white sugar
¾ cup brown sugar
2 tablespoons cornstarch
1 cup boiling water
dash salt
2 tablespoons butter
1 teaspoon vanilla

Cook until thick. Keep at room temperature. Serve warm.

Cal	Prot	Fat	Carb	Fiber	Chol	Sodium
185kc	0g	3g	41g	0g	8mg	39mg

Brown Sugar Sauce (Revised)

Combine white sugar, brown sugar, and cornstarch in a small sauce pan; place over medium-high heat. Gradually add water, stirring constantly until mixture thickens slightly; remove from heat; stir in butter and vanilla.

Yield: 8 (¼ cup) servings

½ cup granulated sugar
½ brown sugar
2 tablespoons cornstarch
1 cup boiling water
2 teaspoons margarine
1 teaspoon vanilla

Cal	Prot	Fat	Carb	Fiber	Chol	Sodium
118kc	0g	1g	28g	0g	0mg	19mg

Brown Sugar Raisin Sauce

Follow above revised recipe except add ½ cup raisins; cover and let set for about 10 minutes. Wonderful on gingerbread.

Yield: 8 servings

Cal	Prot	Fat	Carb	Fiber	Chol	Sodium
150kc	0g	1g	36g	0g	0mg	20mg

Sauces

Lemon Raisin Sauce

1 tablespoon cornstarch
½ cup sugar
1 cup boiling water
2 tablespoons lemon juice
2 tablespoons butter
½ cup raisins

Blend sugar and cornstarch, gradually add water, stirring constantly until it boils; boil 1 minute. Remove from heat, add lemon juice, butter & raisins.

Cal	Prot	Fat	Carb	Fiber	Chol	Sodium
124kc	2g	3g	25g	1g	10mg	40mg

Lemon Raisin Sauce (Revised)

Combine sugar and cornstarch in a sauce pan, blending very well. Place over medium heat; while constantly stirring, add water. Continue to stir until mixture boils; boil 1 minute. Remove from heat; add lemon juice, margarine, and raisins.

Yield: 7 (¼ cup) servings

1 tablespoon cornstarch
½ cup sugar
1 cup boiling water
2 tablespoons lemon juice
2 teaspoons margarine
½ cup raisins
2 teaspoons lemon zest*

*Lemon zest is made by carefully grating the lemon skin only; carefully avoid grating the white pithy part of lemon flesh.

Cal	Prot	Fat	Carb	Fiber	Chol	Sodium
106kc	0g	1g	25g	1g	0mg	20mg

Sandwiches

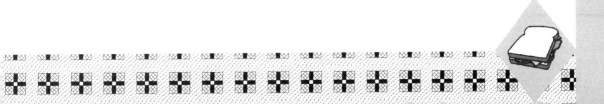

hristmas Eve at my parents' home always found lots of people and more than enough good food. There would usually be 25–35 family members and friends gathered to celebrate the birth of Christ, and we always had great fun. The entire family looked forward to getting together and especially sampling more of Mom's traditional BBQ. She would look forward to this event for weeks. First, she would hang festive Christmas decorations to get in the mood, then she started shopping for gifts. While decorating and shopping, she would manage to address Christmas cards, bake cookies, and make candy—all the things she loved to do. This was, without a doubt, Mom's favorite holiday.

For the Christmas eve party, Mom would provide meat, drinks, various side dishes, and desserts. The other ladies would bring a couple of their favorite side dishes; someone always brought potato salad, someone else brought the green bean casserole, and the assortment of desserts was awesome. My siblings and I all have great memories of the wonderful fellowship, food, laughter, and closeness we shared. Now, Mom's thirteen grandchildren, who always referred to her as "Granny Day," are all grown and scattered. I am happy to say they still have a strong sense of family ties and precious memories of those fun times together.

Granny Day's BBQ Sauce

1 onion, chopped
½ cup tomato catsup
2 cups canned tomatoes
1 tablespoon butter or
   margarine
2 cloves garlic, chopped
½ cup Worcestershire sauce
1 tablespoon sugar
½ cup vinegar
1 tsp soy sauce
red pepper, black pepper,
   salt & mustard

Strain tomatoes, add equal quantity of water, add onion, garlic, catsup, butter, sugar, vinegar, Worcestershire sauce, and soy sauce. Cover; simmer 30 minutes, add seasonings to taste; simmer 30 minutes more or until sauce starts to thicken.

Mom would cook pork loin and rump roasts to use in the sauce. She would wrap each roast separately in aluminum foil, then bake in a slow oven about 325 degrees, until very, very tender. Set roasts aside until almost cool, using 2 forks, shred meat* and mix with barbecue sauce. Place in covered casserole and simmer in slow oven, about 300 degrees for 40–50 minutes or until ready to serve. Serve on sandwich buns with dill pickles.

Yield: approximately 2½ cups sauce or 12 servings

Recipe from: Oma Day

*In certain parts of the South, when BBQ meat is served in this manner, it is called "pulled barbecue."

Cal	Prot	Fat	Carb	Fiber	Chol	Sodium
108kc	2g	3g	22g	2g	0mg	1408mg

Ham Spread

1 lb. chopped ham
1 small jar (4–5 pickles) sweet
    pickles
½ cup mayonnaise, or as
    desired

Grind ham and pickles, mix with mayonnaise

To reduce fat grams and calories use reduced-fat mayonnaise

Yield: 2½ cups

Cal	Prot	Fat	Carb	Fiber	Chol	Sodium
136kc	6g	11g	4g	0g	34mg	508mg

Mary Lib's Barb-Q Ham Sandwiches

Combine first 4 ingredients in sauce pan, heat to bubbling, reduce heat and add ham, simmer at least 10 minutes.

Yield: 6–8 sandwiches

Recipe from: Mary Lib

*Ask your deli to shave ham into very thin slices.

12 oz. chili sauce
1 cup packed brown sugar
¼ cup vinegar
2 scant teaspoon dry mustard
1 lb. chip chopped ham*
6–8 sandwich buns

Cal	Prot	Fat	Carb	Fiber	Chol	Sodium
281kc	12g	7g	184g	2g	7mg	1182mg

Sandwiches

Smoked Turkey Spread

4 cups smoked turkey
2 hard boiled eggs
¼ cup sweet relish
½–¾ cup reduced fat
mayonnaise

Grind turkey in food processor, add chopped boiled eggs, sweet relish and mayonnaise to taste, add sweet pickle juice if spread is too stiff. This is also very good using chicken.

Yield: 4 cups or enough for 16 sandwiches

Recipe from: Larry and Carol Long

Cal	Prot	Fat	Carb	Fiber	Chol	Sodium
124kc	10g	8g	2g	<1g	58mg	123mg

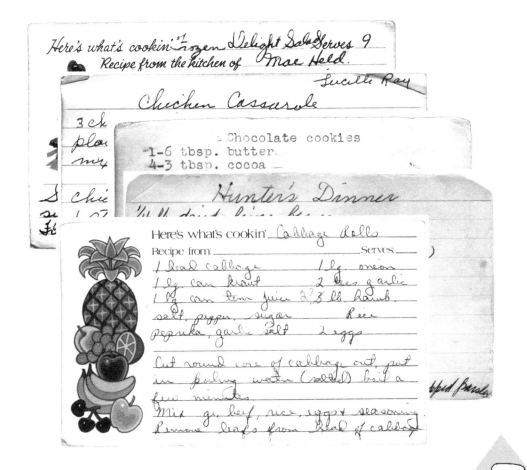

Here's what's cookin' Frozen Delight Salad Serves 9
Recipe from the kitchen of Mae Held.

Lucille Ray
Chicken Casserole

3 ck
pla
my

Chocolate cookies
1-6 tbsp. butter
4-3 tbsp. cocoa

S chi

Hunter's Dinner

Here's what's cookin' Cabbage Rolls
Recipe from: _____ Serves: _____
1 head cabbage   1 lg. onion
1 lg. can kraut   2 cloves garlic
1 lg. can tom. juice   2-3 lb. hamb.
salt, pepper, sugar   Rice
paprika, garlic salt   2 eggs

Cut round core of cabbage out, put
in boiling water (salted) boil a
few minutes.
Mix gr. beef, rice, eggs & seasoning.
Remove leafs from head of cabbage

Desserts

Desserts

Our grandparents had to rely on sweets from their own kitchen to satisfy their sweet tooth. Consequently, when Grandma had the time and the ingredients to spare, she was often in the kitchen making the family's favorite desserts. I remember my Grandma Dowell had a pie safe. This was a wooden cabinet of sorts, with either screen on front and/or sides, or it could be punched tin. They kept the desserts along with other things in the pie safe, to keep it safe from insects. Oh, how I wish I had Grandma's pie safe today!

Looking back, it is interesting to realize how important sweets were to our social time; not only to our friends but also a very important part of the fun times within our own family. In my family, two of our favorite evening entertainments were making fudge or donuts. For John's family, it was fudge and ice cream. It was a very common occurrence to invite friends over for a piece of freshly baked pie or cake. Of course, in those days, you had a lot of "drop-in company." People didn't call ahead; if they were in the vicinity, they would just "drop-in." It was always nice to have some kind of sweets to offer them. For the older children, when your friends visited we would often play records, roll back the rugs and dance, play board games, work jigsaw puzzles or make fudge.

I remember cold winter nights when my mom would make homemade donuts; what a special treat for us children. We would all gather around as Mom mixed the batter and turned it out on a floured surface. From this point, she would encourage us to help roll out the dough, but there were specific ways of doing it. We had to keep a gentle touch and, if we got too heavy handed, someone else was always ready to take over the dough rolling job. While the shortening was heating in a large deep skillet, Mom would let us cut out the doughnuts. When the shortening was just the right temperature, Mom would carefully place the doughnuts in the hot grease; watching them closely. As they floated to the top, you knew they were done. Just as they are turning a golden brown, Mom would carefully lift them from the oil onto a cooling rack that was resting in a pan to catch the dripping fat. Once they were cool, the children were permitted to sprinkle powdered sugar over them, then they were finally ready to eat. Yum, yum! This was one of our favorite winter treats.

Doughnuts

Place about four cups sifted flour in mixing bowl. Make nest in flour, and in it place, 1 cup (heaping) sugar, ½ teaspoon salt, level teaspoon soda, 2 eggs, slightly beaten, 1 teaspoon vanilla and ¼ teaspoon cinnamon (if desired), and 1 cup buttermilk.

Work and mix into a smooth dough. Using all flour is not necessary. Roll on floured board to ½ inch thickness. Cut with doughnut cutter, and fry in very deep fat. Test temperature of fat by dropping small bit of dough into fat. If it comes quickly to surface of fat drop in doughnuts (do not crowd). Turn doughnuts with fork but do not pierce them allowing fat to penetrate doughnuts.

This is a delicious old recipe but I would recommend making a few changes in the directions.

1. Place about 3½ cups flour in bowl to begin with, add more as needed.
2. Blend all dry ingredients together then make nest and add liquids
3. Definitely use cinnamon
4. I find the doughnuts cook more evenly if I roll the dough thinner than ½ inch, more like ⅛"
5. Drop a small piece of bread in hot oil, if it turns brown in 40 seconds oil is ready.
6. Roll half of the cooked doughnuts in powdered sugar the remainder in granulated sugar.

Yield: 24 donuts

Desserts

PIES

Apple Pie 9"

¾ to 1 cup sugar
3 tblsp flour
¾ tsp cinnamon
⅛ tsp nutmeg
6–7 cups sliced apples
salt
2 tblsp butter
two 9" unbaked pie crust

Combine sugar, flour, cinnamon, nutmeg and salt, mix with apples. Put in 9" crust, dot with butter, cover with top crust. Bake 425 degrees 50–60 minutes.

Recipe from: Eleanor Shriver

Cal	Prot	Fat	Carb	Fiber	Chol	Sodium
340kc	2g	14g	55g	4g	10mg	240mg

Apple Pie (Revised)

Combine sugar, flour, cinnamon, and nutmeg; Toss apples and lemon juice, sprinkle flour mixture over apples tossing to coat apples. Spoon into bottom crust, dot with margarine. Make slits in top crust, carefully fold in quarters and place over apples, unfold. Seal top and bottom crust, flute edges. Bake in a 425 degree oven 50–60 minutes or until crust is browned and apples are bubbly and tender.

Yield: 8 servings

*I prefer Macintosh, Jonathan, Cortland or an all purpose apple for my pies.

¾ to 1 cup sugar
3 tablespoons all-purpose
   flour
¾ teaspoon cinnamon
⅛ tsp nutmeg
6–7 cups sliced apples*
1 tablespoon lemon juice
1 tablespoon margarine
two 9" unbaked pie crust

Cal	Prot	Fat	Carb	Fiber	Chol	Sodium
330kc	2g	12g	55g	4g	0mg	230mg

Cooking with Grandma and the Girls

When I was a child growing up in Tennessee, my grandmother and aunts would air dry many different fruits and vegetables. Two of our favorites were "shuck beans" and "dried apples." I don't remember the exact process, but I do remember all of us setting on the porch stringing bushels of green beans to be hung to dry and I remember the sliced fruit being placed over a frame, covered with screen wire, then left to dry.

One of Mom's favorite ways of using the dried apples was in fried apple pies. She didn't have a recipe for fried apples pies; it was just a pinch of this and a dab of that. However, I have a friend, Shirley Ballard, who makes her pies in the same way and was willing to share her directions with me.

I realize this recipe is high in fat, but it was such a favorite with our family and with people in the South. I feel it needs to be preserved and hopefully used with discretion. If your family is like mine and really loves fried apple pies, I know you will enjoy making them on special occasions and using the revised recipe more frequently to satisfy their cravings.

Fried Apple Pies

dried apples
sugar
cinnamon
nutmeg
4 cups all-purpose flour
2 teaspoons salt
1 cup shortening, i.e. Crisco
¾–1 cup cold water
peanut oil

Cover apples with water and cook until tender, this will take 2–3 hours, or cook in microwave. When soft and fairly dry, add sugar, cinnamon and nutmeg as desired.

Pour peanut oil into a deep kettle, or deep fryer about 3″ deep. Heat on low watching carefully not to overheat.

Mix flour and salt, add shortening; using a pastry blender, cut shortening into flour until particles are the size of peas. Gradually sprinkle with cold water, mixing very lightly with fork until flour is moistened. Pinch off portions of dough and roll into balls about 1″ in diameter. Roll out dough on floured surface to about ⅛″ thick. Spoon about 1 tablespoon sweetened fruit onto each round. Moisten edges with water, fold to form a semicircle, and press edges together with a fork. When oil is about 365 degrees, add 1 or 2 pies and cook until light brown. Drain on paper towel.

Yield: 24 small pies

*Recipe from: Shirley Ballard**

Cal	Prot	Fat	Carb	Fiber	Chol	Sodium
190kc	2g	9g	24g	1g	0mg	590mg

Fried Apple Pies (Revised)

Cover apples with water and cook until tender, this will take 2–3 hours, or cook in microwave. When soft and fairly dry, add sugar, cinnamon, nutmeg, and lemon juice.

Preheat oven to 425 degrees. Roll out dough on floured surface to about ⅛″ thick. Using about a 6″ saucer, cut around edge with knife, spoon about 2 tablespoons sweetened fruit onto each round. Moisten edges with water, fold to form a semicircle, and press edges together with a fork. Brush pies with egg-water mixture and bake in 425 oven for about 20 minutes or until browned and crisp.

½ pound dried, sulfur-free
   apples
water
¼ cup white sugar
⅛ teaspoon cinnamon
1/16 teaspoon nutmeg
1 tablespoon lemon juice
1 recipes of Caroline's pie
   crust dough, see page 172
1 egg, beaten
water

Yield: 12 pies

Cal	Prot	Fat	Carb	Fiber	Chol	Sodium
120kc	2g	6g	15g	4g	10mg	100mg

Apple Crumb Topping

½ cup sugar
¾ cup all-purpose flour
2–3 tablespoons margarine

For a delicious and lower fat alternative to a two crust apple pie, use this topping instead of a top crust. Use the lesser amount of margarine.

Blend with a pastry blender, sprinkle over unbaked apple pie. Bake 450 degrees for 10 minutes, reduce heat and bake 350 degrees for 45–50 minutes.

Yield: 8 servings

Cal	Prot	Fat	Carb	Fiber	Chol	Sodium
116kc	3g	3g	57g	1g	0mg	103mg

Apricot Filling

Shirley Ballard's specialty is apricot fried pies, and while she doesn't have a specific recipe for the filling, I think this will come close to hers.

| 1 pound dried sulfur-free apricots |
| water |
| 3 cup sugar |
| 1 teaspoon margarine |

Proceed to make pies as directed in her fried apple pies recipe on page 162 or baked pies on page 161.

Yield: 24 pies

Cal	Prot	Fat	Carb	Fiber	Chol	Sodium
149kc	1g	0g	36g	1g	0mg	3mg

Butterscotch Pie

Separate egg yolks from egg whites, set aside. Combine brown sugar and cornstarch, set aside. Heat milk to near boiling point. Add egg yolks to sugar mixture, slowly add about ½ cup hot milk stirring constantly. Continuing to stir, slowly add sugar-yolk mixture to remaining milk in pan. Continue to stir constantly until it thickens and comes to a boil. Boil for 1 minute. Remove from heat, add butter and 1 teaspoon vanilla; stir.* Cool slightly before pouring into baked pie crust.

| 3 eggs |
| 1 cup brown sugar |
| 3 tablespoons cornstarch |
| 2 cups reduced-fat milk |
| 2 tablespoons butter |
| 1½ teaspoons vanilla, divided |
| one 9" baked pie crust |
| ½ teaspoon cream of tartar |
| ½ cup granulated sugar |

Meringue:

Preheat oven to 350 degrees. Using high speed of electric mixer; beat egg whites and cream of tartar until they start to form peaks. Gradually add granulated sugar, beating well until stiff peaks form, add remaining ½ teaspoon vanilla. Spread meringue over filling; bake in 350 degree oven 8–10 minutes or until meringue is lightly browned. Cool completely before serving.

Yield: 8 servings

Recipe from: Eleanor Shriver

*Can use microwave directions given on page 167 for graham cracker pie filling.

Cal	Prot	Fat	Carb	Fiber	Chol	Sodium
320kc	5g	10g	53g	0g	80mg	190mg

Desserts

Chocolate Pie

6 tablespoons cornstarch, rounded
1 cup sugar
3½ tablespoons cocoa
pinch salt
4 cups milk
4 eggs, separated & beaten
2 teaspoons vanilla
one 9″ pie crust, baked

Combine sugar, cocoa, salt & cornstarch; add beaten egg yolks & milk. Cook until thick, stirring continuously. Remove from fire, add vanilla. Put in baked 9″ pie crust.

Top with meringue or Cool Whip.

Preheat oven to 325 degrees.

Meringue: Beat 4 egg whites until soft peak forms, gradually add 6 tablespoons sugar; beat until egg whites hold a firm peak; stir in vanilla. Spread over top of hot pie filling. Bake in 325 degree oven 10–12 minutes or until brown.

Yield: 8 servings

Recipe from: Betty Mougey

*To reduce fat grams and calories, use 2% milk instead of whole.

Cal	Prot	Fat	Carb	Fiber	Chol	Sodium
300kc	8g	10g	46g	<1g	100mg	190mg

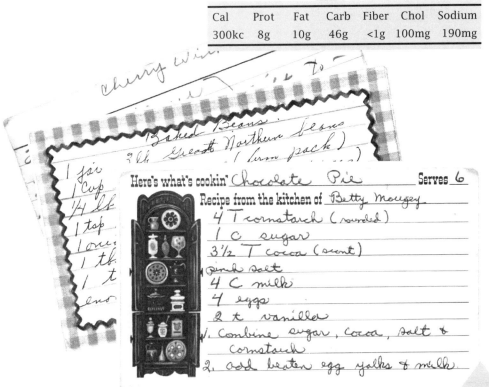

This is probably the most popular of all the desserts Mom Shriver made, she was known throughout the community for her graham cracker cream pie and coconut cream pie. One of the most cherished birthday memories of my husband, John, is about his traditional birthday pie, graham cracker cream. Several years ago, when John's physician suggested he eat a low-fat, low-cholesterol diet, I modified this recipe and made it for his birthday. The next year, John said to me, in a very serious mood, "don't make my graham cracker cream pie this year, if I can't have it the original way, I'd rather do without." Guess what John now gets for his birthday? The original version of his very favorite pie. Below I have presented the recipe in its original form as I received it from Mom Shriver. For the sake of clarity, I have added a few basic instructions enclosed in parenthesis.

Graham Cracker Cream Pie

⅓ cup melted oleo margarine
pinch of sugar
14 graham crackers (this
       means 14 single square
       crackers)

Crust:

Roll crackers into crumbs and mix with oleo and sugar. Save about 2 tablespoons of graham cracker crumbs to put on top of meringue, press remainder in a 9″ pie plate, bake 350 degrees for 5 minutes.

Cream Filling:

(Combine sugar and cornstarch, set aside. Heat milk in saucepan to near boiling point. While milk is heating; add yolks to sugar mixture, slowly add about ½ cup hot milk stirring constantly. While stirring milk in saucepan, slowly add sugar-yolk mixture, continue to stir constantly until it thickens and comes to a boil. Boil for 1 minute. Remove from heat, add vanilla, cool slightly before pouring into baked pie crust.*)

¾ cup sugar
3 tblsp cornstarch
2 cups milk
2 egg yolks, set egg whites
      aside
1 tsp vanilla

See next page for meringue and cream filling microwave directions.

Meringue:

2 egg whites
¼ tsp cream of tartar
¼ cup sugar
1 tsp vanilla.

Preheat oven to 350 degrees. Beat egg whites and cream of tartar in electric mixer until soft peak forms. Gradually add sugar, continuing to beat until egg whites form a stiff peak. Stir in vanilla and spread over cream filling; sprinkle remaining 2 tablespoons graham cracker crumbs on top. Bake in 350 degree oven until meringue is slightly browned.

Yield: 8 servings

Recipe from: Eleanor Shriver

*Cream Filling (Microwave Instructions)
Combine sugar and cornstarch, blending well, set aside. In a 2-quart microwave-safe dish, heat milk 2 minutes on high. Add sugar mixture, mixing well, microwave 4 minutes on high; stirring after 2 minutes. Stir about ½ cup of hot mixture into beaten egg yolks. Continuing to stir; add yolk mixture to remaining milk mixture. Microwave 1–2 minutes on high, stirring about every 30 seconds. Mixture should be thick; remove from microwave, add vanilla.

Cal	Prot	Fat	Carb	Fiber	Chol	Sodium
330kc	5g	12g	50g	0g	50mg	310mg

Next to Mom Shriver's graham cracker pie, her coconut cream pie was undoubtedly the most popular dessert with family and friends. She would usually make an extra pie just to share with someone who needed a little love pat or to make a friend's day a little brighter.

Mom Shriver's Coconut Cream Pie

Mom Shriver didn't have a specific coconut cream pie recipe, she simply made the same cream filling as the graham cracker pie and poured it into a baked 9″ pie crust.

She would then spread meringue over the filling and then sprinkle a generous amount (about ⅓ cup,) of grated coconut on top. She would then brown in a 350 degree oven just until brown.

My mom made hers basically the same way, except she would add about ½ cup shredded coconut to the cream filling and also sprinkle more over the meringue before browning in the oven.

Yield: 8 servings

Cal	Prot	Fat	Carb	Fiber	Chol	Sodium
340kc	6g	14g	55g	<1g	55mg	200mg

Cooking with Grandma and the Girls

Mable's Egg Custard Pie

4 slightly beaten eggs
½ cup sugar
¼ tsp salt
1 tsp vinilla (sic)
2½ cup milk, scalded
one 9" pie shell

Thoroughly mix eggs, sugar, salt and vinella (sic). Slowly stir in hot milk. At once pour into unbaked shell, dust top with nutmeg. Bake 475 degrees 5 minutes, reduce to 425, bake 10 minutes or longer, until set.

Cal	Prot	Fat	Carb	Fiber	Chol	Sodium
295kc	33g	14g	33g	0g	148mg	295mg

Mable's Egg Custard Pie (Revised)

Beat eggs and egg substitute with a wire whisk until frothy, add remaining ingredients, except pie crust and nutmeg. Pour into unbaked pie crust,* dust top with nutmeg. Bake 450 degrees 5 minutes, reduce to 375, bake 30 minutes or longer, until set. To test, insert a table knife into the custard; if it comes out clean, the custard is done.

2 slightly beaten eggs
½ cup egg substitute
½ cup sugar
dash salt
1 teaspoon vanilla extract
2½ cups reduced-fat
 milk, scalded
one 9" unbaked pie crust
dash nutmeg

Yield: 8 servings

*To make custard puddings; pour mixture into custard cups. Place filled cups on a towel in a pan. Pour about an inch of hot water into the pan. Bake in a 325 degree oven for 40–50 minutes until set and a knife comes out clean.
Yield: 8 servings

Recipe from: Mable Bodenhorn

Cal	Prot	Fat	Carb	Fiber	Chol	Sodium
278kc	7g	12g	33g	0g	74mg	244mg

Desserts

Mom's Pumpkin Pie

This is my mom's recipe, which she used for as long as I can remember. The spices made it slightly different from everyone else's. For health reasons, I revised her recipe many years ago, the difference is so slight that it would be hard to detect, and my family has never noticed the difference.

1½ c. cooked pumpkin
1 c. cream
¾ c. sugar
¼ tsp. salt
¼ tsp. nutmeg
¼ tsp. cinnamon
2 eggs, slightly beaten
1 tblsp. butter
1-pie crust

Mix all together and pour into a pie crust. Bake 425 degree oven for 45 minutes. Top each serving with a dollop of whipped cream.

Recipe from: Oma Day

Cal	Prot	Fat	Carb	Fiber	Chol	Sodium
315kc	5g	14g	38g	<1g	85mg	269mg

Mom's Pumpkin Pie (Revised)

Using a wire whisk; combine pumpkin, eggs, sugar, salt, nutmeg, cinnamon, margarine, and cream in a large mixing bowl. Pour into unbaked pie crust, lightly sprinkle with more nutmeg and cloves. Bake 425 degree oven for 45 minutes until the center seems set; test with a table knife; if it comes out clean, it's done. Serve with reduced fat nondairy whipped topping.

Yield: 8 servings

1½ cups cooked pumpkin
1 egg, + 2 egg whites, beaten
    slightly
¾ cup sugar
dash salt
¼ teaspoon nutmeg
¼ teaspoon cinnamon
½ tablespoon margarine
1 cup skim evaporated milk
one 9″ unbaked, pie crust
dash cloves
reduced-fat nondairy whipped
    topping, optional

Cal	Prot	Fat	Carb	Fiber	Chol	Sodium
287kc	6g	10g	41g	<1g	35mg	222mg

Desserts

Raisin Pie

¾ cup sugar
½ tsp. cinnamon
¼ tsp. ground cloves
¼ tsp. salt
3 eggs, separated
1 tblsp. vinegar
1 tblsp. butter, melted
1 c. raisins
¼ c. chopped nuts
one 8^2 pie crust

Mix sugar and spices, add egg yolks, vinegar, butter, raisins and nuts, mix well. Beat egg whites until stiff but not dry; fold into first mixture. Pour into pastry shell. Bake 325 degrees for 40 minutes. Serve with whipped cream.

Cal	Prot	Fat	Carb	Fiber	Chol	Sodium
280kc	4g	11g	44g	2g	75mg	220mg

Raisin Pie (Revised)

Preheat oven to 325 degrees.

Combine sugar and spices, add 2 egg yolks, vinegar, butter, raisins and nuts; set aside. Beat 3 egg whites until stiff but not dry; fold into first mixture. Spoon into pie crust. Bake 325 degrees for 40–50 minutes or until set.

Serve with reduced fat nondairy whipped topping.

Yield: 8 servings

¾ cup sugar
½ teaspoon cinnamon
¼ teaspoon ground cloves
dash salt
2 eggs, + 1 egg white, separated
1 tablespoon vinegar
1 tablespoon margarine, melted
1 cup raisins
2 tablespoons chopped nuts
one 8" pie crust
nondairy whipped topping

Cal	Prot	Fat	Carb	Fiber	Chol	Sodium
260kc	3g	9g	43g	2g	45mg	150mg

Desserts

Desserts

The secret to flaky pie crust is to have all your liquids cold, work the dough as little as possible and quickly as possible. Roll it out with a light touch and handle very gently.

Two Crust Pie Pastry

> 2 cups sifted all-purpose flour
> ¾ teaspoon salt
> ⅔ cup hydrogenated shortening, (Crisco, Spry, etc.)
> ¼ cup cold water

Mix flour and salt, add shortening; with a pastry blender, cut shortening into flour until particles are the size of peas. Gradually sprinkle with cold water, mixing very lightly with fork until flour is moistened. Roll into ball, divide into two portions, roll out on a lightly floured surface for crust, or wrap with plastic wrap and store in refrigerator until ready to use. Roll about 1″ larger then pan, fold pastry into quarters and carefully transfer to pie pan, unfold. Fit pastry into pan, trim ragged edges and crimp or flute edges of crust, hooking parts of crust under pan rim.

If making a baked pie crust:

Make pastry following above recipe. Prick pastry with a fork to prevent puffing during baking. Bake in 475 degree oven for 8–10 minutes or until brown. If pastry puffs up, prick puffs with fork. Fill with filling according to your recipe.

Frozen Pie Crust:

Make pastry following above recipe; roll out according to above directions. Place pastry in pie pan, fit a piece of plastic wrap down onto crust. Place pan in a large zip-lock bag; remove as much air as possible, zip tight and place in freezer. When ready to use; proceed with pie recipe; no need to thaw.

Yield: 16 servings

Cal	Prot	Fat	Carb	Fiber	Chol	Sodium
130kc	2g	9g	12g	0g	0mg	110mg

Cooking with Grandma and the Girls

The following recipe is a healthier alternative, which you will find is still nice and flaky.

Caroline's Pie Crust

2⅔ cup flour
1 tsp. salt
⅔ cup oil
4 tblsp cold water

Blend with fork; roll into a smooth ball. Roll each ball between two pieces of waxed paper. Fold pastry in quarters; carefully transfer to pie pan. Makes two 9″ pie crust.

Yield: 16 servings

Recipe from: Caroline Shriver

Cal	Prot	Fat	Carb	Fiber	Chol	Sodium
160kc	2g	9g	16g	<1g	0mg	150mg

Graham Cracker Crust

Combine all ingredients, press in a 9″ pie pan, save a little crumbs for topping. Bake in 350 degree oven for 5 minutes.

Yield: 8 servings

1⅓ cups graham cracker
crumbs (7 double crackers)
3 tablespoons sugar
⅓ cup butter, melted

Cal	Prot	Fat	Carb	Fiber	Chol	Sodium
140kc	1g	9g	14g	<1g	21mg	138mg

Graham Cracker Crust (Revised)

1⅓ cups graham cracker
crumbs
1 tablespoon sugar
¼ cup margarine, melted

Combine all ingredients, stirring with a fork until all maragrine is absorbed. Reserve 2 tablespoons mixture to sprinkle on top of pie. Press remaining mixture in bottom and up sides of 9″ pie pan. Bake in 350 degree oven for 5 minutes.

Yield: 8 servings

Cal	Prot	Fat	Carb	Fiber	Chol	Sodium
108kc	1g	7g	11g	<1g	0mg	105mg

Desserts

PUDDING

Apple Pudding

4 cups diced apples

2 eggs

2 cups sugar

1 tsp vinella (sic)

½ cup Crisco

2 cups flour

¾ tsp salt

1 tsp soda

1 tsp baking powder

2 tsp cinnamon

1 cup chopped nuts

Break eggs over apples, cream sugar, vanilla and Crisco, Sift flour, add all dry ingredients, add to sugar & Crisco. Stir in apple mixture. 9×13 pan. Bake 1 hour at 325 degrees.

Cal	Prot	Fat	Carb	Fiber	Chol	Sodium
230kc	3g	10g	34g	1g	20mg	210mg

Apple Pudding Cake (Revised)

Preheat oven to 350 degrees; spray a 9×13 baking pan with vegetable spray.

In a large mixing bowl, mix cream, sugar, and margarine; add eggs and vanilla. In a small bowl combine flour, salt, soda, baking powder, and cinnamon; gradually add dry ingredients to sugar mixture alternating with milk; beat well after each addition. Fold in nuts and apples; spoon into prepared baking pan. Bake in 350 degree oven for 50–55 minutes, or until a wooden pick comes out clean.

Yield: 20 servings

This can be served with brown sugar sauce, page 149, whipped topping, or ice cream.

vegetable spray

2 cups sugar

½ cup margarine

1 egg + 2 egg whites or
    ½ cup egg substitute

1 teaspoon vanilla extract

2 cups all-purpose flour

dash salt

1 teaspoon baking soda

1 teaspoon baking powder

2 teaspoon cinnamon

½ cup reduced-fat milk

¼ cup chopped nuts

4 cups diced apples

Cal	Prot	Fat	Carb	Fiber	Chol	Sodium
200kc	3g	6g	34g	<1g	10mg	160mg

Upside-Down Date Pudding

1½ cups dates, cut up
1¼ cups boiling water
¾ cup white sugar
¾ cup brown sugar
2 eggs
3 tablespoon butter or margarine, melted
2¼ cup sifted flour
1½ tsp soda
¾ tsp baking powder
¾ tsp salt
1½ cup nuts
1 recipe Brown Sugar Sauce

Combine dates and water. Blend sugar, eggs and butter. Sift together dry ingredients; add sugar mixture. Stir in nuts and cooled dates mixture. Pour into pan. Top with brown sugar sauce.

Recipe from: Eleanor Shriver

Cal	Prot	Fat	Carb	Fiber	Chol	Sodium
330kc	4g	9g	61g	2g	25mg	250mg

Brown Sugar Sauce:

Pour over date cake, bake in moderate oven 375 about 40 mins. Cut in squares, invert on plate. Serve warm with whipped cream.

Combine:
2¼ cup brown sugar
1½ tablespoons butter or margarine
2 cups boiling water

Upside-Down Date Pudding (Revised)

1½ cup dates, cut up

1¼ cup boiling water

2¼ cup sifted all-purpose flour

1½ teaspoon baking soda

¾ teaspoon baking powder

¼ teaspoon salt

3 tablespoons margarine

½ cup granulated sugar

½ cup brown sugar

2 eggs

¼ cup chopped pecans or
   walnuts

Sauce:

1½ cups brown sugar

1 tablespoon margarine

2¼ cups boiling water

reduced-fat nondairy whipped
   topping, optional

In a medium bowl combine dates and boiling water, set aside to cool.

Preheat oven to 375 degrees; spray a 9×13 pan with vegetable spray.

Combine flour, baking soda, baking powder and salt, set aside. In a large mixing bowl, beat margarine, white and brown sugar until creamy. Beat in eggs, one at a time. Add dry ingredients, beat about 1 minute. Stir in cooled date mixture and nuts. Spoon into prepared baking pan. Combine sauce ingredients, pour over batter. Bake in 375 degree oven about 35–38 minutes or until wooden pick comes out clean. Cut in squares, invert on plate. Serve warm with whipped cream.

Yield: 20 servings

Cal	Prot	Fat	Carb	Fiber	Chol	Sodium
230kc	3g	4g	47g	1g	20mg	190mg

Desserts

Cottage Pudding

This recipe came from my quilting friend, Bobbi Mason. She has wonderful memories about her grandmother in Massachusetts making it and how special it was to the grandchildren. Bobbi's great-grandmother was Emma Davis Hunter, an Indian in Massachusetts.

Cottage pudding was a favorite for our grandmothers. Therefore, there are many versions. I think it was so popular because it used only basic ingredients which they would have kept on hand.

1 cup sugar
dash nutmeg
1½ cups flour
salt
2 teaspoons baking powder
¾ cup milk
1 tablespoon butter
vanilla
1 egg
Sauce:
1 cup sugar
2 cups boiling water
2 tablespoons cornstarch
4 tablespoons butter
2 teaspoons vanilla
½ teaspoon salt

Combine sugar, butter, and egg. Combine flour, nutmeg, salt, and baking powder. Gradually add milk and vanilla alternating with dry ingredients until blended. Beat 1–2 minutes.

Bake in a 9×9 greased and floured pan. 375 degrees for 30 minutes.

Sauce: Combine sugar, cornstarch and salt, add water, bring to a boil. When thick remove from heat; add butter and vanilla.

Recipe from: Bobbi Mason

Cal	Prot	Fat	Carb	Fiber	Chol	Sodium
330kc	4g	8g	63g	<1g	40mg	320mg

Cottage Pudding (Revised)

vegetable spray
2 cups sugar, divided
3 tablespoons margarine,
  divided
1 egg
3 teaspoons vanilla extract,
  divided
1½ cups all-purpose flour
dash nutmeg
dash salt
2 teaspoons baking powder
¾ cup reduced-fat milk
2 tablespoons cornstarch
2 cups boiling water

Preheat oven to 375 degrees; spray a 9×9 pan with vegetable spray. In a medium mixing bowl cream 1 cup sugar, 1 tablespoon margarine, egg, and 1 teaspoon vanilla. In a small bowl combine flour, nutmeg, salt, and baking powder. Gradually add dry ingredients, alternating with milk; beat on medium-high 2 minutes. Bake in a 9×9 greased and floured pan. 375 degrees for 30 minutes.

Sauce: Combine remaining sugar, cornstarch, and salt in small saucepan, blend very thoroughly. Place over medium-high heat, stirring constantly; add boiling water; continue to stir until mixture thickens slightly. Remove from heat; add remaining margarine and vanilla, stirring well.

Yield: 9 servings

To serve: Cut cake into squares, place in individual dishes, spoon about 3 tablespoons sauce over cake.

Cal	Prot	Fat	Carb	Fiber	Chol	Sodium
310kc	3g	4.5g	63g	<1g	20mg	180mg

Mom's Bread Pudding

This was a family favorite with the Shrivers, and now our grandchildren, Joe, Jenny and Sara, love it.

4 eggs, beaten well
1 pt milk
¾ cup sugar
1 tsp vanilla
add about 2 cups bread,
    broken into small pieces
add ½ cup raisins
Sprinkle with nutmeg

Bake about 45–60 minutes. Test with knife.

Recipe from: Eleanor Shriver

Cal	Prot	Fat	Carb	Fiber	Chol	Sodium
263kc	7g	7g	41g	1g	194mg	181mg

Mom's Bread Pudding (Revised)

Spray a 2-quart baking dish with vegetable spray. Remove crust from bread and tear into marble size pieces. Spread the bread in bottom of prepared baking dish. Using a wire whisk, beat eggs and egg substitute until frothy. Add milk, sugar, vanilla, cinnamon, salt, and raisins. Pour over the bread crumbs. Let stand for about 15–20 minutes while bread absorbs the liquid. Sprinkle with nutmeg.

While bread is soaking, preheat oven to 350 degrees. Bake pudding in 350 degree oven for 45–60 minutes until center is firm and knife comes out clean when tested. To serve, spoon into individual dessert bowls, pour a small amount of milk over top and serve immediately. Also good with vanilla sauce (page 148).

vegetable spray
4–5 slices stale white bread
2 eggs, beaten well
½ cup egg substitute
1½ cups reduced-fat milk
½ cup fat-free half-and-half
¾ cup sugar
1 teaspoon vanilla extract
½ teaspoon cinnamon
dash salt
½ cup raisins
dash nutmeg

Yield: 6 servings

Cal	Prot	Fat	Carb	Fiber	Chol	Sodium
276kc	7g	4g	45g	1g	96mg	266mg

Banana Pudding

Vanilla wafers bring back memories of my mom's banana pudding. Our family loved it so much she would make at least a double recipe of cream pudding and a whole box of vanilla wafers. This is not my mom's original recipe, I don't think she ever had one, but this is the way she made it and it tastes just like hers.

2 cups milk*
1 cup sugar,* divided
3 tablespoon cornstarch
2 egg yolks
2 teaspoon vanilla extract, divided
½ box vanilla wafers
3 bananas, ripe but not brown
2 egg whites
¼ cup sugar

Scald milk. Blend ¾ cup of sugar and cornstarch, add yolks. Stirring slowly, add about ½ cup hot milk to sugar mixture. While stirring, slowly add sugar mixture to remaining milk in pan. Continue to stir constantly until it thickens and comes to a boil. Boil for 1 minute.** Remove from heat, add 1 teaspoon vanilla, cool slightly. Pour about ½ cup into a 2-quart baking dish, layer with vanilla wafers, slice bananas over wafers. Continue until all pudding is used.

Preheat broiler.

Meringue:

Beat egg whites until foamy, gradually add remaining ¼ cup sugar. Beat until stiff peak forms, add remaining 1 teaspoon vanilla. spread on top of pudding. Brown quickly under broiler to prevent bananas browning.

Yield: 8 servings

*To reduce calories and fat grams; substitute reduced-fat milk and reduce sugar to ¾ cup total.
**See Graham Cracker Cream Pie, page 167 for microwave instructions.

Cal	Prot	Fat	Carb	Fiber	Chol	Sodium
360kc	5g	9g	66g	2g	60mg	160mg

CAKES

Our ancestors, living in remote areas, had to make many adjustments in their lifestyles. To survive, they had to have some knowledge of medicine, husbandry, farming, carpentry, textiles, sewing, etc. The list goes on and on. Not only did they need the knowledge, they also had to make adjustments for materials and supplies. In cooking, many of the spices, condiments, and other ingredients they were familiar with "back home," were not available. This necessitated changes in old recipes, resulting in the creation of many new ones. Supposedly, the apple stack cake is one of these creations. As the story goes, it is similar to a popular dessert of stacked cakes and sweetened fruit which was popular in their British homeland. However, in their new home, these supplies were either scarce or simply not available. The mountain women of the Appalachian region, in Tennessee, Kentucky, and the Carolinas, "making do" with supplies on hand, created this marvelous cake, which has become a very important part of our epicurean culture. Even to this day, you can go to a church reunion or a funeral wake in this region and you may find at least one of these cakes being served.

My maternal grandparents, William and Hannah (Ray) Dowell, were referred to by their children as Mommy and Poppy. Consequently, the grandchildren called them Mommy and Poppy Dowell. They lived their life in the Appalachian mountains of Tennessee and Kentucky and raised eight children there. I always loved to hear my mother tell about growing up in these mountains. Her father, Poppy Dowell, worked for a coal mining company and would be sent into a region where the site of a new mine was to be located. Once Poppy Dowell had established a home for his family, he would proceed to clear certain areas of trees. He would then cut the trees into timbers, which would be used to shore up the mineshafts. My grandparents lived a very hard life—and, I would imagine, a lonely one for Mommy Dowell. I know she loved the Lord, from whom I'm sure she gained her strength. I know she was creative in her quilts and she loved to garden. Judging from stories I have heard about the food she cooked, I feel certain she must have also been creative in her cooking as well. My actual memories of my Mommy Dowell are rather vague. She was a tiny woman, who was always kind and soft-spoken. Mommy and Poppy Dowell were able to spend their last years on earth living in town near us. Here they could spend their days on the front porch in their rocking chairs, where they would visit with or at least wave to their neighbors as they passed by.

One of Mommy Dowell's specialties was an apple stack cake and any reference to this cake was always, "Mommy's apple stack cake." When she was no longer able to cook, her youngest daughter, my Aunt Hattie, carried on the tradition of baking this family favorite, and I think her cakes are the best I ever ate. Aunt Hattie would generously share her cakes with the family, but they were always referred to as, "Mommy's apple stack cake."

The ingredients for this special cake were recorded in my mom's ancient cookbook, but no details on quantities, baking time, etc. This was not a problem for our grandmas because they all knew how much flour to add to get the batter to just the right consistency. They knew to make it into 9 thin layers and bake until just the right degree of brown and until the cake pulled away from the pans. The apple filling, which was made from their own dried apples, was prepared by taste. The women would rinse them to get rid of any dust or bugs; then they would cook them in a little water, sweetened with sugar and cinnamon with maybe a touch of nutmeg. The apples were then spread between the layers of cake, stacked, covered, and left to set in the "spring house" along with milk and butter for at least three days before eating. The longer it set, the moister it became.

When I approached Aunt Hattie about my dilemma, she graciously shared her portions, and all her secrets. One point she kept stressing was to not use sulfur-dried apples, only the naturally dried. Her only request was that I pass the recipe on to the younger generations.

Mommy Dowell's Apple Stack Cake

½ cup butter

1½ cup sugar

2 eggs, beaten

2 teaspoons vanilla

3¼ cups all-purpose flour, or more

2 teaspoons baking powder

½ teaspoon baking soda

½ teaspoon salt

½ cup buttermilk

6 cups dried apples*

sugar

cinnamon

nutmeg

Preheat oven to 350 degrees. Grease & flour four 9″ round cake pans.

Cream butter & sugar until light and fluffy, add eggs and vanilla, beating well. Combine flour, baking powder, baking soda, and salt; gradually add to creamed mixture, alternating with buttermilk. Mix well after each addition. Add more flour if necessary to achieve a dough thick enough to work with. Divide the dough into 9 equal portions, press dough evenly over the bottom of each prepared cake pan. Bake in 350 degree oven about 10–12 minutes or until brown and crusty looking, and the edges pull away from the pan. Cool on wire racks for 5 minutes; turn out on racks and cool completely. Continue until all dough is used. At this point, the layers may be wrapped, sealed in airtight plastic bags and frozen for several weeks.

Place dried apples and just enough water to prevent sticking to pan in a medium sized saucepan Bring to a boil over medium heat; reduce to low and simmer for about 15–20 minutes or until fruit is tender and not too juicy.** Remove from heat, add sugar according to taste, cinnamon and nutmeg, cool completely. Spread filling evenly over each layer, stacking layers as you go. Cover and allow to set over night before refrigerating, refrigerate at least 2 days before serving.

Yield: 20 servings

Recipe from: Hattie Hale

*Most dried apples you purchase today have been treated with sulfur in the drying process, Sulfur apples require lengthy cooking time, if they don't want to cook soft, you can use a potato masher to help speed the process. Even though they don't cook up as tender and they also turn very dark, the taste is fine. I prefer to purchase sulfur-free dried apples in a health food store, or you could dry your own.

**If apples do not absorb enough moisture, add applesauce until desired consistency.

I did not think it was necessary to revise this recipe.

Cal	Prot	Fat	Carb	Fiber	Chol	Sodium
250kc	3g	5g	48g	3g	30mg	220mg

Frozen Cocoanut (sic)* Pound Cake

3 sticks oleo
3 cups sugar
6 eggs
1 teaspoon cocoanut (sic) flavoring
1 package frozen cocoanut (sic)
¼ teaspoon salt
¼ teaspoon soda
1 cup sour cream
1 teaspoon vanilla
3 cups flour

Cream butter and sugar, add eggs, beat well. Add flavoring then flour, salt and soda. Alternating with sour cream. Fold in cocoanut (sic). Bake at 250 degrees for one hour or until tester comes out clean.

*I found this spelling in numerous old cookbooks.

Cal	Prot	Fat	Carb	Fiber	Chol	Sodium
564kc	6g	28g	83g	3g	123mg	284mg

Frozen Coconut Pound Cake (Revised)

Combine 1 cup sour cream, coconut and coconut flavoring; refrigerate for 2–3 days before making cake.

Preheat oven to 350 degrees; grease and flour 2 loaf pans or 1 tube pan.

Cream margarine and sugar, add eggs and egg substitute, beating well after each addition, add the remaining ½ cup sour cream and vanilla flavoring, beat well.

In a small bowl combine flour, salt and soda, gradually add to creamed mixture, alternating with sour cream-coconut mixture, beat on low speed until smooth. Spoon into prepared pans. Bake at 350 degrees for 60 to 70 minutes for loaf pans or 80–90 minutes for tube pan, or until tester comes out clean. Cool on rack for 10 minutes before inverting cake onto rack; cool completely.

1¼ cups reduced-fat sour cream*
½ cup frozen or fresh coconut
1 cup margarine
3 cups sugar
3 whole eggs
¾ cup egg substitute
1½ teaspoons coconut extract
½ teaspoon vanilla extract
3 cups all purpose flour
¼ teaspoon soda
¼ teaspoon salt

Yield: 14 servings

*To reduce fat grams and colaries, use fat-free sour cream.

Cal	Prot	Fat	Carb	Fiber	Chol	Sodium
452kc	6g	18g	68g	3g	64mg	218mg

Peach Pound Cake

3 cups flour
¼ teaspoon soda
¼ teaspoon salt
½ cup sour cream
1 teaspoon vanilla
1 teaspoon almond
1 cup margarine
3 cups sugar
6 eggs
2 cups fresh or frozen peaches,
    chopped

Preheat oven to 350 degrees; grease and flour 10″ tube pan.

In a medium bowl combine flour, soda, and salt; in a small bowl combine sour cream, vanilla, and almond flavoring. Cream margarine and sugar, add eggs, beating well after each one. Add sour cream mixture, beat well. Gradually add flour mixture, beating well, stir in peaches. Spoon into tube pan. Bake in 350 degree oven for 75–80 minutes.

Recipe from: Princetta MacLaren

Cal	Prot	Fat	Carb	Fiber	Chol	Sodium
440kc	6g	17g	67g	1g	85mg	280mg

Peach Pound Cake (Revised)

Preheat oven to 350 degrees; grease and flour 10″ tube pan.

In a medium bowl combine flour, baking soda, and salt. In a small bowl combine sour cream, vanilla, and almond flavoring. Cream margarine and sugar; gradually add eggs and egg substitute, beating well after each addition. Add sour cream mixture, beat well. Gradually add flour mixture, beating well, stir in peaches. Spoon into tube pan. Bake in 350 degree oven for 80–90 minutes, or until long pick comes out clean.

Yield: 14 servings

3 cups all-purpose flour
¼ teaspoon baking soda
dash salt
½ cup + 2 tablespoons
    reduced fat sour cream
1 teaspoon vanilla extract
1 teaspoon almond flavoring
¾ cup margarine
3 cups sugar
3 whole eggs
¾ cup egg substitute
2 cups fresh or frozen peaches,
    chopped

Cal	Prot	Fat	Carb	Fiber	Chol	Sodium
400kc	7g	11g	68g	1g	40mg	200mg

Desserts

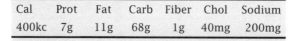

Desserts

Judy's Cheese Cake

14 graham crackers, crushed
to make crumbs

⅓ cup melted margarine.

Mix, pat into 10″ spring form
pan.

Bake at 350 degrees 5 min. Or
make without crust:

⅔ cup sugar

1 lb cream cheese

⅛–½ tsp almond flavoring

3 eggs

Recipe from: Judy Morris

Combine above ingredients and beat until smooth. Pour into baked crust or well-buttered 10″ pie plate. Bake 350 degrees for 25 minutes. Cool 20 minutes.

1–2 cups sour cream
1–2 tsp vanilla
5–6 tblsp sugar

(If you are using a pie pan, use the lesser amounts; for a 10″ spring form pan, use the greater amounts.) Mix well and pour over top of cream cheese mixture. Bake 350 degrees for 10–20 minutes. Cool, cover, refrigerate. Freezes very well.

Cal	Prot	Fat	Carb	Fiber	Chol	Sodium
380kc	6g	23g	37g	<1g	85mg	360mg

Judy's Cheese Cake (Revised)

Preheat oven to 350 degrees. Combine cracker crumbs and margarine, press into a 10″ spring form pan, or a 10″ pie pan. (You can also make this cheesecake using no crust.) Bake in 350 degree oven 5 minutes.

Combine ⅔ cup sugar, cream cheese, almond extract and eggs; beat by hand until smooth. Do not over beat. Pour into baked crust or well-buttered 10″ pie plate. Bake 350 degree oven for 25 minutes. Cool 20 minutes. Combine sour cream, vanilla and sugar, *(If you are using a pie pan, use lesser amounts; for a 10″ spring form pan use the greater amounts.) Mix well; pour over top of baked cream cheese mixture. Return to 350 degree oven and bake for 10–20 minutes. Cool, cover, refrigerate. This freezes very well.

14 single graham crackers,
crushed

¼ cup melted margarine.

⅔ cup sugar

1 lb reduced fat cream cheese

⅛–½ tsp almond extract, as
desired

3 eggs

1–2 cups reduced fat sour
cream*

1–2 tsp vanilla*

5–6 tblsp sugar*

Yield: 14 servings

Cal	Prot	Fat	Carb	Fiber	Chol	Sodium
310kc	8g	13g	40g	<1g	60mg	350mg

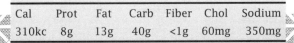

White Cocoanut (sic) Cake

(This was a common spelling for coconut in many of the old books.)

8 oz. sour cream
12 oz. fresh or frozen cocoanut
2½ cups granulated sugar, divided
1 cup powdered sugar
½ cup butter
2½ cups sifted cake flour
1 tsp salt
2½ tsp baking powder
1 cup sweet milk
½ tsp vanilla
1 teaspoon cocoanut flavoring
4 egg whites, beaten stiff

Mix sour cream, cocoanut (sic), 1 cup granulated sugar and 1 cup powdered sugar; refrigerate for 3 days. Cream butter and remaining 1½ cups sugar until creamy. Sift cake flour, salt, and baking powder. Add flour mixture to butter and sugar, alternating with milk and flavoring. Carefully fold in egg whites. Pour into greased & floured 9″ pans, bake 30–35 minutes at 350 degrees. After cooling, divide halves with thread making 4 layers. Put sour cream mixture in between layers and on top of cake (or whipped cream can be put on top and sides. Put cocoanut (sic) on top. Let set in refrigerator 3 days.

Recipe from: Jean Sasseen

Cal	Prot	Fat	Carb	Fiber	Chol	Sodium
340kc	4g	14g	52g	2g	25mg	260mg

White Coconut Cake (Revised)

Prepare cake mix according to package directions, adding ½ teaspoon coconut extract. You can make two 9″ round cakes or one 9×13 cake. Cool thoroughly. If making round layers; divide each layer, using thread, making four layers. Combine sour cream, sugar, ¼ cup coconut, remaining coconut extract, and whipped topping; spread between layers, stacking layers carefully as you work, put remaining mixture on top and sides. Sprinkle remaining coconut over top. Place in covered cake plate and refrigerate 1–3 days, the longer it sets, the better it gets.

1 (18 oz.) white cake mix
1 cup reduced fat sour cream
¾ cup sugar
½ cup shredded coconut
1½ teaspoons coconut extract
2½ cups reduced-fat nondairy whipped topping

Yield: 20 servings

Cal	Prot	Fat	Carb	Fiber	Chol	Sodium
190kc	2g	6g	31g	0g	5mg	180mg

Desserts

Date & Nut Cake

6 ½ oz. pkg. dates, finely cut
1 cup hot water
½ cup butter or soft shortening
1 cup sugar
1 egg
1 teaspoon vanilla
1 ¾ cup sifted flour
1 teaspoon soda
½ teaspoon salt
½ cup nuts, chopped

Pour hot water over dates, cool. Combine shortening, sugar, eggs & vanilla in mixing bowl, beat 5 minutes until fluffy. Sift together flour, soda, salt, add alternately in four additions with date mixture, blend until smooth. Add nuts & pour into greased & floured pan. Bake 350 degrees 40–45 minutes.

Recipe from: Oma Day

Cal	Prot	Fat	Carb	Fiber	Chol	Sodium
370kc	5g	15g	60g	3g	59mg	238mg

Date & Nut Cake (Revised)

Preheat oven to 350 degrees; spray a 9×9″ baking pan with vegetable spray.

Pour hot water over dates; set aside to cool. Combine margarine and sugar in a large mixing bowl; add egg and vanilla, beat well. Combine flour, baking soda, and salt, add to creamed mixture, alternating with date mixture; beat well after each addition. Stir in nuts; pour into prepared baking pan. Bake 350 degrees 40–50 minutes, or until a wooden pick comes out clean.

Cool slightly, sprinkle lightly with powdered sugar.

Yield: 9 servings

vegetable spray
8 oz. pkg. chopped dates
1 cup hot water
⅓ cup margarine
1 cup sugar
1 egg
1 teaspoon vanilla extract
1¾ cup all-purpose flour
1 teaspoon baking soda
⅛ teaspoon salt
¼ cup nuts, chopped

Cal	Prot	Fat	Carb	Fiber	Chol	Sodium
181kc	4g	7g	60g	3g	30mg	166mg

Grandma's Sunshine Cake

1½ cup sugar
½ cup water
6 eggs beaten separately
¼ teaspoon salt
1 cup cake flour
¾ teaspoon cream of tartar

Boil sugar and water until threads, pour the hot syrup in a fine stream on the beaten egg whites to which salt has been added, beating well till cool. Add well beaten egg yokes, (sic) sift flour once, measure, add cream of tartar, fold carefully into egg mixture add extract.

Recipe from: Grandma Carrie Detar

Note: Nutritional data does not include a glaze.

Cal	Prot	Fat	Carb	Fiber	Chol	Sodium
170kc	4g	2.5g	83g	0g	137mg	150mg

Grandma's Sunshine Cake (Revised)

Sift together flour, salt, and baking powder; set aside. Combine water, 1 teaspoon orange flavoring and vanilla, set aside. Beat egg whites and cream of tartar until stiff; set aside. Beat egg yolks thoroughly, gradually add sugar. Gradually add dry ingredients, alternating with liquids; fold in beaten egg whites. Pour into ungreased tube pan. Bake in 325 degree oven 60 minutes or until top springs back when touched. Invert pan over a bottle or funnel until cool. When cool: Combine powdered sugar, margarine, orange juice and remaining orange flavoring; beat until smooth. Drizzle over top of cooled cake; sprinkle orange zest over top.

Yield: 12 servings

1½ cup cake flour
¼ teaspoon salt
1 teaspoon baking powder
⅓ cup water
1½ teaspoon orange extract, divided
1 teaspoon vanilla extract
6 eggs beaten separately
1 teaspoon cream of tartar
1½ cups sugar
2 cups sifted powdered sugar
1 tablespoon melted margarine
3 tablespoons fresh orange juice
zest from 1 large orange*

*Zest is the gratings of the colorful outer coating of citrus fruits, otherwise known as grated rind, use only the colored portion of skin.

Note: Nutritional data includes glaze.

Cal	Prot	Fat	Carb	Fiber	Chol	Sodium
270kc	4g	3.5g	104g	0g	137mg	140mg

Lazy Daisy Cake

As a child I remember this being a traditional Christmas dessert, but any time we could persuade my mom to bake it was a special occasion. Following is Mom's original recipe, I thought about trying to make a revision, but the luscious richness is the unique quality of this cake.

2 eggs
1 cup sugar
4 tblsp melted butter
1½ squares of chocolate
1 cup sifted flour
1 tsp baking powder
½ tsp salt
½ cup milk, scalded
1 tsp vanilla

Melt butter & chocolate in the top of a double boiler, set aside to cool.

Beat eggs until lemon colored, add sugar gradually, beating well; stir in cool butter-chocolate mixture. Add dry ingredients gradually, alternating with lukewarm milk, beating well after each addition. Stir in vanilla. Pour into greased & floured 9×9 cake pan. Bake 30 min at 350 degrees. When cake is done add frosting:

Frosting:

Cook together until medium thick, pour on cake, put under broiler until coconut is a delicate brown and bubbly.

1 cup coconut
1 cup brown sugar
⅛ lb. butter or margarine (4 tablespoons)

Yield: 12 servings

Recipe from: Thelma Crumley, my mom's cousin

Cal	Prot	Fat	Carb	Fiber	Chol	Sodium
320kc	3g	13g	49g	<1g	45mg	280mg

Cooking with Grandma and the Girls

This was always a favorite for special occasions at the Shrivers; you could always count on having Mom's raisin bars.

When our children were small, we lived about 300 miles from John's parents. We could normally leave late in the evening, driving into the wee hours of the morning in order to not lose a day's work and yet arrive at the Shrivers in time to catch a few hours sleep before all the festivities began. As we would approach the area where they lived, I would think of these spicy, chewy, delicious bars waiting in the kitchen for a little snack to tide us over until breakfast. I was not disappointed too many times!

Raisen (sic) Bars

Boil together for 20 min.:

1 box of raisens (sic)

2½ cups water

1 cup of shortening

Sift together in large bowl:

4 cups flour

2 cups sugar

2 tsp soda

2 tsp cinnamon

1 tsp cloves

1 tsp salt

Add to dry ingredients:

2 eggs

1 cup of chopped nuts

Add raisens (sic) to mixture & beat well. Spread batter in two large greased & floured cake pans. Bake at 350 degrees for 12–15 min. Ice with powdered sugar frosting.

Recipe from: Eleanor Shriver

Cal	Prot	Fat	Carb	Fiber	Chol	Sodium
370kc	5g	15g	58g	3g	20mg	260mg

Desserts

Desserts

Raisin Bars (Revised)

vegetable spray
8 oz. raisins
1¼ cups water
½ cup margarine
2 cups all-purpose flour
1 cups sugar
1 teaspoons baking soda
1 teaspoons cinnamon
½ teaspoon ground cloves
dash salt
1 teaspoon vanilla extract
1 egg
¼ cup chopped nuts
2 cups powdered sugar, sifted
1 tablespoon soft margarine
2 teaspoons orange juice
2 teaspoons lemon juice

Preheat oven to 350 degrees; spray a 9×13 pan with vegetable spray.

Combine raisins, water, and margarine, bring to a boil over medium-high heat; reduce heat and simmer about 20 minutes. Combine flour, sugar, baking soda, cinnamon, cloves, and salt in a large mixing bowl. Add raisin mixture liquid to flour mixture; beat. Add egg, beating well; continue to beat about 2 minutes, stir in raisins. Spread batter into prepared cake pan. Bake at 350 degrees for 27–28 minutes or until a wooden pick comes out clean.

To frost: Combine powdered sugar, margarine, orange and lemon juice, mix well, beat until smooth. Spread on cooled raisin bars.

Yield: 20 bars

Cal	Prot	Fat	Carb	Fiber	Chol	Sodium
220kc	2g	7g	39g	1g	10mg	140mg

Desserts

Japanese Fruit Cake

This was a traditional Christmas dessert in the Day family. It takes lots of ingredients and time, but don't be intimidated, the end result is more than worth the time and effort. Also, remember that it yields 2 cakes.

White Layer:

1½ cups sugar
½ cup butter
6 egg whites
3 cups flour
dash salt
3 tsp baking powder
1 cup sweet milk

Yellow Layer:

1½ cup sugar
½ cup butter
6 egg yolks
3 cups flour
3 tsp baking powder
1 tsp cinnamon
1 tsp cloves
1 tsp allspice
1 cup sweet milk
1 box raisins

Frosting:

3 grated coconuts
4 lemons
3 ½ cups sugar
3 cups hot water
4 tblsp flour

White Layer: Cream sugar & butter together, add egg whites. In a small bowl combine flour, salt & baking powder, add flour ½ cup at a time to sugar mixture alternately with milk. Beat on medium speed for 2 minutes. Pour into 3 greased & floured 9″ cake pans. Bake 350 for 40 minutes.

Yellow Layer: Cream sugar & butter together, add egg yolks. In a small bowl combine flour, baking powder. cinnamon, cloves and allspice, add flour mixture ½ cup at a time to sugar mixture alternating with milk. Beat on medium speed for 2 minutes. Pour into 3 greased & floured 9″ cake pans. Bake 350 for 40 minutes.

Frosting: Mix lemon juice & sugar, add flour, add hot water and cook until thick enough to spread, grate coconut and sprinkle over cake.

Recipe from: Oma Day

Cal	Prot	Fat	Carb	Fiber	Chol	Sodium
440kc	6g	17g	71g	4.5g	45mg	155mg

Up until about four years ago, I had never made this recipe because the result was two 3-layer cakes. I would wishfully think about it occasionally, but I was never willing to put forth the time and effort to revise the recipe to yield just one cake. As I thought about recipes from my mom that I would like to include it in this book, I immediately thought of this recipe, this was just the nudge I needed to start working on a revision. I am very pleased with the results and now you can enjoy a wonderful dessert without worrying about what to do with that second cake.

Japanese Fruit Cake (Revised)

vegetable spray
1 cup margarine
2 cups sugar
4 eggs
3½ cups all-purpose flour
2 teaspoons baking powder
1 cup reduced-fat milk
1 teaspoon vanilla
1 teaspoon cinnamon
½ teaspoon ground cloves
1 teaspoon ground allspice
2 cups raisins

Preheat oven to 350 degrees; spray three 9″ round cake pans with vegetable spray.

Cream margarine and sugar; add eggs one at a time, beating well after each addition. In a small bowl, sift flour and baking powder; gradually add to creamed mixture alternating with milk, beating well after addition. Add vanilla; beat on medium speed for about 1 minute. Pour one-third of mixture into one prepared pan. Add cinnamon, cloves, and allspice; blend well. Stir in raisins; pour remaining mixture into 2 pans. Bake at 350 degrees for 30–35 minutes or until a wooden pick comes out clean. Cool in pans for about 5 minutes; invert on racks and cool completely before frosting.

Yield: 20 servings

Cal	Prot	Fat	Carb	Fiber	Chol	Sodium
450kc	5g	16g	77g	3g	40mg	220mg

3 tablespoons
 all-purpose flour
2 cups sugar
1 cup boiling water
juice from 2 lemons
zest of 2 lemons*
1 (6 oz.) pkg. shredded
 coconut
½ cup chopped pecans
pecan halves to garnish

Lemon-Coconut Frosting:

Thoroughly blend flour and sugar in a medium saucepan, add lemon juice, stir. Place over medium-high heat, while stirring, add boiling water. Stir frequently until mixture starts to thicken, about 10 minutes. Remove from heat; stir in coconut and nuts. Cool. Prick layers slightly with a fork, place one spice cake layer on plate, spread ⅓ frosting over it, proceed using the yellow layer, ⅓ frosting and remaining spice layer. Spread remaining frosting on top of cake. Garnish with pecan halves; cover. This is best when left to set at least 24 hours.

Yield: 20 servings

*Zest is the gratings of the colorful outer coating of citrus fruits, otherwise known as grated rind, use only the colored portion of skin.

FROSTING AND ICINGS

Fluffy White Frosting

The Shriver kitchen always had cookies in the little green cookie jar and usually a pie or cake for the family or maybe to take to a friend who needed a little cheer.
    The family's favorite cake was chocolate cake with this white fluffy frosting.

Stir sugar, water and syrup together in a saucepan; cover and bring to a boil. Remove lid and cook until syrup spins a long thread about 230 degrees. While syrup is cooking beat egg whites until stiff. Slowly pour hot syrup in a thin stream into beaten egg whites, continue beating until frosting is stiff, add vanilla and continue to beat until it looses its glossy appearance. Will frost a 2-layer 9″ cake or one 9×13 cake.

½ cup sugar
2 tablespoons water
¼ cup light Karo syrup
2 egg whites
1 teaspoon vanilla

Yield: will frost a cake to serve 20

Recipe from: Eleanor Shriver

Cal	Prot	Fat	Carb	Fiber	Chol	Sodium
35kc	0g	0g	8g	0g	0mg	10mg

7-Minute Cake Frosting

This was and still is my favorite recipe for white frosting. I have never seen it fail.

2 egg whites
1½ cups sugar
¼ teaspoon cream of tartar or 1 tablespoon Karo syrup
⅓ cup water
1 teaspoon vanilla

Combine all ingredients except vanilla in top of a double boiler. Have water boiling in bottom of double boiler, but not enough for it to touch bottom of top pan. Beat with electric mixer until mixture is stiff and stands in a peak when tested. Add vanilla, beat until it looses its glossy appearance.
    Will frost a 2-layer 9″ cake or one 9×13 cake.

Yield: will frost a cake to serve 20

Cal	Prot	Fat	Carb	Fiber	Chol	Sodium
60kc	0g	0g	15g	0g	0mg	5mg

Caroline's Good Powdered Sugar Icing

The success of this frosting is the amount of fat and the excessive beating. Therefore, I won't try to revise it, I would suggest you save this for special occasions and enjoy it in its original form.

Cream oleo & Crisco using a mixer, until fluffy. Gradually add sugar, vanilla and milk, beat very well. When desired consistency; spread over your favorite cake.

Good on chocolate, banana, or carrot cake.

Yield: will frost a cake to serve 20

Recipe from: Caroline Shriver

1 stick oleo (margarine) room
 temperature
1 tblsp Crisco, (or other solid
 hydrogenated shortening)
1 lb. box powdered sugar
1 tsp vanilla
milk- just enough to moisten

Cal	Prot	Fat	Carb	Fiber	Chol	Sodium
140kc	0g	5g	23g	0g	10mg	45mg

Caramel Frosting

Melt margarine, add brown sugar; bring to boil over low heat, stirring constantly. Add milk, continue stirring until mixture comes to a boil, remove from heat; cool slightly.

Add powdered sugar until spreading consistency.

Yield: will frost a cake to serve 20

Good on spice or chocolate cake.

½ cup margarine
1 cup brown sugar
¼ cup milk
4 cups powdered sugar

Cal	Prot	Fat	Carb	Fiber	Chol	Sodium
180kc	0g	4.5g	35g	0g	0mg	65mg

Mocha Frosting

Beat all together until spreading consistency, may need to add more sugar or cream.

Yield: will frost a cake to serve 20

Good on chocolate cake.

2½ cups powdered sugar
½ cup cocoa
4 tablespoons strong cold coffee
2 tablespoons margarine
2 tablespoons cream
dash salt

Cal	Prot	Fat	Carb	Fiber	Chol	Sodium
80kc	0g	2g	16g	<1g	0mg	15mg

Desserts

CANDY

When I was a youngster and we had friends over, fudge making was the highlight of the evening. Whether we had a friend or two over for the evening or spending the night, we would end up in the kitchen making fudge. My first attempts at fudge making were not altogether successful. After experiencing several batches of soupy candy, which you had to eat with a spoon, I paid more attention to the details. You soon learned just exactly what my mom meant when she used the term, "firm ball," "hard crack," etc. Her instructions were to begin with a large iron skillet,* because when the candy starts to boil, it can easily boil over. She also had us use a long-handled spoon, because the mixture splatters and spits as it bubbles. After it boiled for a period of time, she said to fill a tea cup with very cold water, dip your cooking spoon into the syrupy mixture, then drizzle some over the cold water. We didn't mind frequent testing because the tester got to taste the samples. When the fudge had cooked to the desired stage, we poured it into a greased pan or plate to cool. The cooling period was really a test of patience, as we struggled against the temptation to sample the finished product right away. In all honesty, it is still a very difficult thing for me to do even today!

Following are a few common terms used before everyone had a candy thermometer on hand.

*You can use any heavy bottomed skillet or pan, it should be about 4 times as large as the volume of candy.

230–234 degrees =	spins a fine thread, or hair when dropped from a spoon
234–238 degrees =	soft ball, syrup forms a soft ball when drizzled from tip of spoon into cold water but disintegrated when rolled around with fingers
238–244 degrees =	medium firm, syrup forms a little firmer ball when dropped in cold water
244–248 degrees =	firm ball, syrup holds its shape when drizzled into water and holds shape when picked up with fingers
248–254 degrees =	hard ball, syrup forms an more rigid ball, but still pliable
254–265 degrees =	very hard ball, syrup forms an even more rigid ball
265–285 degrees =	soft crack, syrup drizzled into cold water will separate into threads which are pliable
290–300 degrees =	hard crack, syrup drizzled into cold water form hard brittle threads and will make a cracking sound when tapped against side of cup

Chocolate Fudge

This is my mom's old recipe which she always made in a large cast iron skillet.

Mix 3 cups sugar & 3 large spoons cocoa until mixed good. Mix 1 cup cream & cook until a soft ball will form, then put in 2 Hershey bars, 1 spoon vanilla & a piece of butter about 1½" long & beat until thick and pour into greased dish.

Recipe from: Oma Day

Chocolate Fudge (Revised)

3 cups sugar
3 tablespoons cocoa
1 cup evaporated milk
2 Hershey bars
1 teaspoon vanilla
1 tablespoon butter
chopped nuts, optional

Using a large heavy pan, combine sugar and cocoa; blending completely. Add milk, stir until sugar is dissolved. Cover, bring to a boil, uncover, reduce heat to medium-low and cook without stirring until candy thermometer registers 240 degrees, or it forms a soft ball when dropped into cold water. Remove from heat, add Hershey bars, butter, and vanilla; do not stir. Set in a shallow pan of cold water until outside of pan is cool. Add nuts if desired; beat until it starts to thicken, spoon into a buttered 9×9 pan. Cool slightly before cutting into squares.

Yield: sixty-four 1" pieces

Recipe from: Oma Day

Cal	Prot	Fat	Carb	Fiber	Chol	Sodium
50kc	0g	.5g	11g	0g	0mg	10mg

Chocolate Fudge

2 cups sugar
2 tlbsp cocoa
2 tblsp Karo syrup
¾ cup evaporated milk
1 tblsp butter
1 tsp vanilla

Cook till firm ball in cold water. Set aside, add butter and vanilla. Let cool then beat till it starts to harden add nuts.

Revised instructions: Follow instructions for my mom's fudge.

Yield: thirty-six 1″ pieces

Recipe from: Eleanor Shriver

Cal	Prot	Fat	Carb	Fiber	Chol	Sodium
60kc	0g	0g	13g	0g	0mg	10mg

Peanut Butter Fudge

Using a large heavy pan, combine sugar and milk, stir until sugar is dissolved. Cover, bring to a boil, uncover, reduce heat to medium-low and cook without stirring until candy thermometer registers 234 degrees, or it forms a soft ball when dropped into cold water. Remove from heat add peanut butter, and vanilla; do not stir. Set in a shallow pan of cold water until outside of pan is cool. Add nuts; beat until it starts to thicken, spoon into a buttered 8×8″ pan.

2 cups sugar
½ cup milk
2 tablespoons light corn syrup
⅓ cup peanut butter
1 teaspoon vanilla
chopped nuts or raisins,
    optional

Yield: sixty-four 1″ pieces

Recipe from: Oma Day

Cal	Prot	Fat	Carb	Fiber	Chol	Sodium
35kc	0g	.5g	7g	0g	0mg	10mg

Peanut Butter Rolls

This is a favorite from my childhood, and I passed it on to our children and grand-children. I'm not sure if they like it so well because of the taste or if it's the novelty of eating candy made from cold mashed potatoes. This recipe is sometimes referred to as potato candy. My mother made hers a little differently, but I have made this recipe for years.

½ cup cold mashed potatoes

4–5 cups sifted powdered sugar, or more

⅛ teaspoon salt

1 teaspoon vanilla

1½ cups smooth peanut butter

In a medium bowl combine cold potatoes, salt, vanilla and powdered sugar. Add more sugar if necessary to make dough easy to handle. Divide dough in half: roll out the dough into a rectangle shape, less than ¼″ thick on a lightly dusted surface. Lightly spread half the peanut butter over the dough; roll up jellyroll fashion. Repeat, using the remaining dough. Refrigerate until firm, slice about ½″ thick to serve.

Yield: approximately forty-eight ½″ slices

To store: Wrap securely in plastic wrap. Keeps well in refrigerator for several days or for weeks in freezer.

Cal	Prot	Fat	Carb	Fiber	Chol	Sodium
80kc	2g	4g	10g	<1g	0mg	50mg

Desserts

Divinity

Divinity played a large role in the Shrivers's holiday traditions. Mom Shriver always had plenty on hand at Thanksgiving and Christmas, and for Easter she would make her divinity Easter eggs. To make the Easter eggs, she would shape a portion of the divinity into egg shapes then dip them in melted Hershey chocolate bars, Everyone would have their own divinity Easter egg, a great treat which we all looked forward to. John was stationed in Okinawa with the Air Force during Christmas of 1962 and not very happy at the prospect of spending Christmas away from his family. We were all trying to cheer him up by sending him gifts and his special holiday treats from home. I was sending lots of cookies so Mom Shriver thought her divinity would be the perfect goodie to send him. She lovingly made the candy, adding lots of candied fruit and nuts; cut it into even little pieces then lovingly packed it in a box, between layers of waxed paper and using more waxed paper to cushion the precious cargo. I love to hear John tell how excited he was to receive the package from his mom knowing it would be some special homemade treat. Alas, when he opened the box, the divinity was all in one large lump in the bottom of box. When he was able to stop laughing, he proceeded to break off pieces and savor each morsel. He claims it was the best divinity he had ever eaten!

3 cups sugar

½ cup white Karo

½ cup water

2 egg whites

1 tsp vanilla

walnuts & candied
    fruit, if desired

Put sugar, Karo and water in pan, cover with lid, boil until it spins a hair. While syrup is boiling, beat egg whites till stiff. Pour ½ the syrup into well beaten egg whites, beating as you pour. Continue cooking remaining syrup till it cracks against cup when dropped into cold water, pour into egg whites. Add vanilla and beat until it looses its gloss. Work in nuts & cherries, if desired and turn onto buttered 9×13 pan.

Yield: 40 pieces

(If divinity doesn't want to set up in bowl, add powdered sugar until desired consistency.)

Cal	Prot	Fat	Carb	Fiber	Chol	Sodium
70kc	0g	0g	18g	0g	0mg	10mg

Divinity Easter Eggs

Divinity Easter eggs were a traditional part of Easter in the Shriver household. Mom was always so faithful in making a divinity egg for each person in the family. This was really a special treat for the grandchildren.

Make divinity as above, add nuts, cherries or whatever fruit desired. Shape into egg shapes, let cool. Melt Hershey's chocolate bars in top of double boiler, CAREFULLY, cover candy eggs with chocolate, let dry on a wire rack.

Recipe from: Eleanor Shriver

COOKIES

The Green Cookie Jar

Mom Shriver kept a green pottery cookie jar (filled of course,) on her cupboard for years. The kids always complained that they could never sneak a cookie because, when you raised or replaced the lid, it would "clink." Little did the children realize or even care that this cookie jar was such a nostalgic part of their mom's life and would be to future generations.

The first few years of Mom and Dad Shriver's married life, they lived in Oklahoma, Pennsylvania. At that time, they had to walk down to the river and across the bridge into Apollo, which was about three miles, to shop for whatever they needed. This was in the late 1920s and early 1930s when the stores would have certain promotions to entice people to shop with them. Depression glass as well as numerous pottery items are some of the great collectibles of today that came from that era. One enticement was the accumulation of points with the amount of the receipts saved, depending on how much they spent at one particular store. Mom Shriver would patronize a particular market in Apollo and save her receipts for special gifts. Then, when she had accumulated the required number of receipts, she chose a very special green cookie jar with a little decal on the side. The storekeeper carefully wrapped the cookie jar in brown paper and Mom Shriver carried this newly acquired treasure the three miles back to their home in Oklahoma. This little green cookie jar was in continuous use for over sixty years.

After John's father died, the little green cookie jar was given to him and it now resides in our home in Texas. It has a little crack, looks a little faded and worn, and it doesn't coordinate with our blue decor; but it has its own spot on our kitchen countertop. It is not always filled with cookies, but when the children and grandchildren come home for a visit I make a point of filling it with fresh home baked cookies, and I know Mom Shriver, who is watching from heaven, gets a big smile on her face every time she hears one of her loved ones "clink" that old cookie jar.

Caramel Cookies

4 eggs
1 cup butter
4 cups brown sugar
1 tsp salt
1 tsp soda
1 tsp baking powder
1 tsp vanilla
6 tblsp water
6 cups flour
1 cup nuts

(There were no directions for this recipe.)

Cal	Prot	Fat	Carb	Fiber	Chol	Sodium
80kc	2g	4g	8g	0g	15mg	85mg

Caramel Cookies (Revised)

Preheat oven to 350 degrees; spray cookie sheets with vegetable spray.

Cream butter and sugar in a large mixing bowl; add eggs, beating well after each one. Add vanilla, mix well. Combine flour, soda, and baking powder; gradually add to creamed mixture, alternating with water, beating well after each addition. Stir in chopped nuts. Drop by teaspoonful onto prepared cookie sheets, bake at 350° for about 9–10 min.

Yield: 72 cookies

vegetable spray
3 eggs +2 egg whites
1 cup margarine
4 cups brown sugar
1 teaspoon salt
1 teaspoon baking soda
1 teaspoon baking powder
1 teaspoon vanilla
6 tablespoons water
6 cups all-purpose flour
½ cup chopped nuts, or less

Cal	Prot	Fat	Carb	Fiber	Chol	Sodium
120kc	2g	3.5g	20g	0g	10mg	100mg

Cherry Winks

When Dad Shriver was asked what kind of cookies he would like, he would reply "Cherry wink."

Sift together:
2¼ cups sifted Pillsbury best enriched flour
1 tsp double-acting baking powder
½ tsp soda
½ tsp salt

Combine:
¾ cup shortening
1 cup sugar, cream well

Blend in:
2 eggs
2 tblsp. milk
1 tsp vanilla

Blend in:
sifted dry ingredients; mix well

Add:
1 cup chopped pecans
1 cup chopped dates
⅓ cup chopped maraschino cherries

Mix well. Shape into balls using a level tablespoon of dough for each cookie. Crush 2½ cups Kellogg's corn flakes. Roll each ball of dough in corn flakes. Place on greased baking sheet. Top each cookie with ¼ maraschino cherry. Bake in moderate oven 375, 10–12 minutes. Do not stack or store until cool.

Yield: 5 dozen cookies

Cal	Prot	Fat	Carb	Fiber	Chol	Sodium
80kc	1g	4g	10g	<1g	5mg	40mg

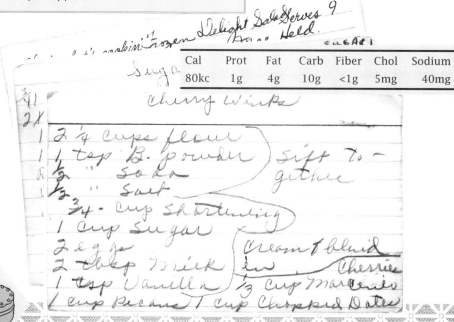

Desserts

Desserts

Cherry Winks (Revised)

2¼ cups all-purpose flour

1 teaspoon baking powder

½ teaspoon baking soda

¼ teaspoon salt

¾ cup margarine

1 cup sugar

2 eggs

1 tablespoon reduced-fat milk

1 teaspoon vanilla

¼ cup chopped pecans or walnuts

1 cup chopped dates

1 cup chopped maraschino cherries, divided

2½ cups corn flakes, finely crush

Preheat oven to 350 degrees; lightly spray cookie sheets with vegetable spray.

Combine flour, baking powder, soda, and salt; set aside. Cream margarine and sugar until fluffy; add eggs, milk, and vanilla, beat well. Gradually add flour mixture to creamed mixture, mix well. Stir in nuts and dates, chop ½ cup cherries and add to mixture. Chill at least 2 hours.

Cut remaining ½ cup cherries in half. Shape dough into balls using a level tablespoon of dough for each cookie. Roll each ball of dough in corn flakes, place on prepared cookie sheet, top with a cherry half. Bake in moderate oven at 375°, 10–12 minutes. Do not stack or store until cool.

Yield: 60 cookies

Cal	Prot	Fat	Carb	Fiber	Chol	Sodium
70kc	1g	3g	12g	0g	5mg	65mg

Desserts

Cooking with Grandma and the Girls

As a new bride, I was always eager to browse through Mom Shriver's cookbooks and recipe box. She had quite a collection of old cookbooks, but the one that always fascinated me was a little brown notebook in which she had written recipes during the early years of her marriage. One day I was upstairs in Dad's office typing recipes and, as I was looking through this little brown book, I saw this recipe and couldn't imagine what these confusing numbers were all about. I immediately went in search of Mom for an explanation, and Mom, in her infinite patience, began to explain. "The numbers in parentheses are the order in which you mix the ingredients; the first set of measurements is for a small batch, the second set of measurements is for a regular batch. You drop by teaspoon onto cookie sheet and bake until done."

I now have this little brown notebook and I cherish it, not only for the memories of Mom, but because inside the covers are little stick people drawn by my husband, John, as a very young child.

Chocolate Cookies

(1) 6 tlb butter	12 tlb (¾ cup)
(4) 3 tlb coca	5 tlb (⅓ cup)
(5) 6 tlb milk	12 tlb (¾ cup)
(3) 2 eggs	4 eggs
(4) ⅓ tsp soda	⅔ tsp
(4) ¼ tsp salt	½ tsp
(6) ¾ cup nuts	1 cup
(2) ¾ cup sugar	1½
(4) 1⅛ cup flour	2¼
(7) (½ tsp vanilla	(1 tsp)

This recipe was found in Mom's little brown book with no directions.

Chocolate Cookies (Revised)

Preheat oven to 350 degrees; very lightly spray cookie sheets with vegetable spray.

In a large bowl, cream margarine, sugar, and cocoa; add eggs and vanilla extract, beating after each addition. Combine flour, soda, and salt; gradually add to creamed mixture, alternating with milk, beating well after each addition; stir in nuts. Drop by teaspoonfuls onto prepared cookie sheets. Bake at 350 degrees for 7–8 minutes or just until firm. Cool before frosting.

Frosting: Sift powdered sugar into mixing bowl; combine remaining margarine, milk, and vanilla; add to sugar. Stir very well until desired consistency to spread, adding more milk or powdered sugar if necessary.

Frost cooled cookies; let set until frosting is firm before packing between sheets of waxed paper.

Yield: 86 cookies

Recipe from: Eleanor Shriver

*I find these cookies do best when frozen and removed from freezer as needed.

½ cup + 2 tablespoons
   margarine
1½ cups sugar
⅓ cup cocoa
3 eggs + 1 egg white
1 teaspoon vanilla extract
2¼ cups all-purpose flour
1 teaspoon baking soda
¼ teaspoon salt
6 tablespoons reduced-fat milk
¼ cup chopped nuts, if desired
Frosting:
3 cups powdered sugar
1 tablespoon reduced-fat
   margarine
2–3 tablespoons reduced-fat
   milk
½ teaspoon milk

Cal	Prot	Fat	Carb	Fiber	Chol	Sodium
45kc	1g	2g	6g	0g	5mg	45mg

Nut rolls were among the favorites of Christmas sweets in the Pittsburgh area where John grew up. Even though they are very high in fat content, I wanted to pass the recipe along with the hope that it will be served as an exceptional treat for a holiday or special occasion.

Nut Rolls

1 lb. butter
1 lb. cream cheese-cream
   together & add:
4 egg yolks
5 cups flour
½ cup sugar

Filling:
5 cups walnuts, ground,
1 cup sugar
4 egg whites, beaten stiff
1 tsp vanilla

Make 72 small balls (I make 144 very small balls), place on wax paper, sprinkled with powdered sugar. Chill for 1 hr. or overnight. Pat down flat on powdered sugar & spread with ½ tsp filling. Roll & bake at 375 for 25 minutes.

Recipe from: Caroline Shriver

Cal	Prot	Fat	Carb	Fiber	Chol	Sodium
170kc	3g	13g	12g	<1g	35mg	75mg

Nut Rolls (Revised)

Cream margarine and cream cheese, add yolks and sugar, gradually add flour; blend well. Cover; refrigerate overnight. Preheat oven to 325 degrees.

Prepare filling by combining nuts, sugar, egg whites and vanilla, set aside.

Divide dough into fourths; using ¼ of dough, roll out on a surface dusted with powdered sugar. Roll to about ⅛″ thick, cut into 3×3 squares, then wedges. Spread with desired filling,* roll up jellyroll style, place on cookie sheets. Bake at 325 degrees for 10 minutes or until brown.

Yield: approximately 72 rolls

12 ounces cream cheese
2 cups margarine
5 cups all-purpose flour
½ cup sugar
2 egg yolks

Filling:
5 cups ground walnuts or
   pecans
1 cup sugar
4 egg whites, beaten stiff
1 teaspoon vanilla extract

*I like to use different kinds of filling for variety, I prefer to make my own nut filling, but you can buy prune, apricot and poppy seed in the grocery.

Cal	Prot	Fat	Carb	Fiber	Chol	Sodium
170kc	3g	12g	12g	<1g	10mg	85mg

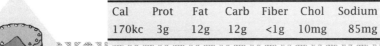

Desserts

John's grandparents, Lincoln and Carrie Detar, lived a simple and good life. They lived just on the outskirts of Oklahoma, a small town in western Pennsylvania, where they could be out in the country with enough land for a few chickens, a cow called Bossie, and large garden. If one arrived unannounced in the summer, it was not unusual to find Grandma at her favorite gardening pastime—working in her strawberry patch. I can still see her with old cotton stockings pulled up over her arms to protect her from insect bites. Oh, how she loved her strawberries and spent many hours weeding and carefully picking the delectable crop.

John and I loved to join Grandma and Grandpa Detar for their favorite lunch, which was "ring bologna" and crackers. Grandma would cut the bologna into cubes and serve it along with saltine crackers and coffee. Grandpa really loved coffee, he would pour it in his saucer to cool, and then carefully slurp it from the saucer. If strawberries were in season, you would have the pleasure of a freshly picked bowl of sweet, juicy strawberries. If not, Grandma always kept homemade cookies in her crockery cookie jar. Her favorite cookies were large and thick ginger cookies, but unfortunately this recipe has been lost. John remembers that, even as a teenage boy, the most he could eat would be three of her huge cookies. While I liked her ginger cookies, my favorite was her orange cookies.

Grandma Detar's Orange Cookies

1 cup shortening
2 cups sugar
3 eggs
grated rind & juice of 2 oranges
1 cup sour milk
1 teaspoon soda
4½ cups flour
2 tsp baking powder

Mix together; bake 350 degrees for 8–9 minutes.

Recipe from: Grandma Carrie Detar

Note: Nutrition data does not include frosting.

Cal	Prot	Fat	Carb	Fiber	Chol	Sodium
70kc	1g	3g	10g	0g	5mg	35mg

Grandma Detar's Orange Cookies (Revised)

Preheat oven to 350 degrees; lightly spray cookie sheets with vegetable spray.

In a large bowl, cream 1 cup margarine and granulated sugar; add eggs one at a time, beating well after each addition; add orange juice and half the orange zest. Combine flour, baking soda, baking powder, and salt; gradually add to creamed mixture, alternating with sour milk, beat well after each addition. Drop by teaspoonfuls onto prepared cookie sheet. Bake in 350 degree oven for 8 minutes or until set. Cool completely before frosting.

Frosting:

Melt remaining 1 tablespoon margarine, combine with powdered sugar, 3 tablespoons milk and remaining orange zest. Stir until smooth, add additional milk until the desired consistency. Frost cookies; let set until frosting is firm, store between sheets of wax paper.

Yield: 90 cookies

vegetable spray
1 cup + 1 tablespoon
    margarine, divided
2 cups granulated sugar
2 eggs + 2 egg whites
zest from 2 oranges,* divided
½ cup orange juice
1 cup sour milk**
4½ cups all-purpose flour
1 teaspoon baking soda
2 teaspoon baking powder
¼ teaspoon salt
2 cups powdered sugar, sifted
3 tablespoons reduced-fat milk
    or more if needed

*Zest is the gratings of the colorful outer coating of citrus fruits, otherwise known as grated rind, use only the colored portion of skin.
**Pour 1 tablespoon vinegar or lemon juice into a 1-cup measuring cup, add enough low fat milk to fill to 1-cup line.

Cal	Prot	Fat	Carb	Fiber	Chol	Sodium
80kc	1g	2.5g	12g	0g	5mg	70mg

Raisin Spice Drop Cookies

3 cups sifted flour
1 tsp. baking soda
1 tsp. salt
1 tsp. cinnamon
½ tsp. cloves
1 cup shortning, (sic)
1½ cup light brown sugar, firm
    pack
3 eggs
1 tsp. venilla (sic)
1 cup chopped walnuts
2 cups raisins

Mix together, bake 8–10 minutes at 350 degrees.

From: Caroline Shriver

Cal	Prot	Fat	Carb	Fiber	Chol	Sodium
70kc	1g	3.5g	10g	0g	5mg	45mg

Raisin Spice Drop Cookies (Revised)

Preheat oven to 350; lightly spray cookie sheets with vegetable spray. Cream margarine and brown sugar; add eggs one at a time, beating well after each addition, add vanilla and apple sauce. Combine flour, baking soda, salt, cinnamon and cloves; gradually add to creamed mixture, beating until smooth. Stir in walnuts and raisins. Drop by teaspoonfuls onto prepared cookie sheets, bake in 350 oven for 8–10 minutes or until set.

Yield: 90 cookies

¾ cup margarine
1½ cups brown sugar
2 eggs +2 egg whites (or
    to equal ¾ cup)
1 teaspoon vanilla extract
3 cups all-purpose flour
1 teaspoon baking soda
dash salt
1 teaspoon cinnamon
½ teaspoon cloves
2 tablespoons apple sauce
⅓ cup chopped walnuts
2 cups raisins

Cal	Prot	Fat	Carb	Fiber	Chol	Sodium
60kc	1g	2g	10g	0g	5mg	40mg

Desserts

Raisin Filled Cookies

These were a favorite in the guy's lunch when they were deer hunting. They are a favorite anytime for my husband John, daughter Audrey, and son Johnnny.

Dough:	Mix, add:	Filling:
1 cup brown sugar	3 eggs	1 cup raisins
1 cup granulated sugar	5 cups flour or less	1 cup brown sugar
1 cup Crisco	1 tblsp. milk	1 cup water
	½ tsp. salt	3 tsp. flour or cornstarch
	2 tsp. vanilla	rounded
	1 tsp. baking powder	
	1 tsp. soda	

Mix ingredients for dough, refrigerate 1–2 hours. Roll dough out fairly thin, cut out with glass or round cookie cutter. Place 1 tbsp. filling in center, top with another circle of dough and pinch edges together.

Cook filling ingredients until thick then cool. (Make twice this much filling, if you like the cookies fat) Bake at 400 degrees 11–12 min.

From: Lil Butler

Cal	Prot	Fat	Carb	Fiber	Chol	Sodium
160kc	2g	5g	28g	<1g	10mg	75mg

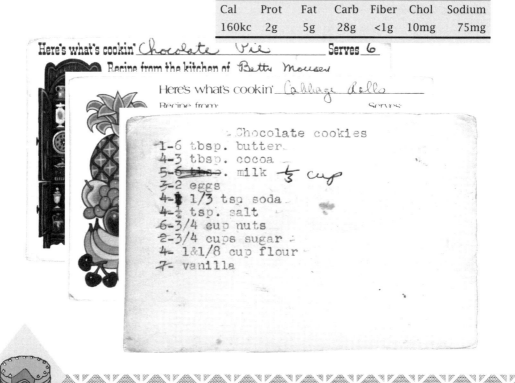

Here's what's cookin' Chocolate Pie   Serves 6

Recipe from the kitchen of Betty Mousser

Here's what's cookin' Cabbage Rolls

Recipe from: Serves

Chocolate cookies
1-6 tbsp. butter
4-3 tbsp. cocoa
5-6 tbsp. milk ⅓ cup
3-2 eggs
4-1 1/3 tsp soda
4-¼ tsp. salt
6-3/4 cup nuts
2-3/4 cups sugar
4- 1&1/8 cup flour
7- vanilla

ur grandchildren love to be included in making any kind of cookies; John Andy and Clay love to help me with this one, and they also love to eat them.

Raisin Filled Cookies (Revised)

Cookie dough:

1 cup brown sugar

1 cup white sugar

1 cup margarine

3 eggs

1 tablespoon reduced-fat milk

4½–5 cups or more
    all-purpose flour, divided

¼ teaspoon salt

2 teaspoons vanilla extract

1 teaspoon baking powder

1 teaspoon baking soda

Filling:

2 cups brown sugar

3 tablespoons corn starch

2 cup water

2 cups raisins

vegetable spray

Cream brown sugar and white sugar with margarine until well blended; add eggs, milk and vanilla, blend well. Combine 4½ cups flour, salt, baking powder and soda; gradually add to creamed mixture, blending well, add more flour as needed. Cover; refrigerate 2 hours or overnight.

Filling:

In a medium saucepan, blend remaining 2 cups brown sugar and 3 tablespoons cornstarch, add water, stir, and add raisins. Cook over medium heat, stirring constantly, until filling thickens; remove from heat and cool.

Preheat oven to 400 degrees; lightly spray cookie sheets with vegetable spray.

Using about ¼ of the dough, roll out on lightly floured surface until fairly thin, about ⅛″ thick. Using a round cookie or biscuit cutter, cut one set of circles; using a slightly larger cutter, cut another set of smaller circles. Place smaller circle on prepared cookie sheet, place about 1–2 tablespoons of raisin filling in center; carefully place a larger circle over raisin filling. Pinch edges of dough with fingers or a floured fork to seal. Be careful to seal edges well to prevent the filling from seeping out. Bake at 400 degrees 11–12 minutes.

Yield: 45 cookies, using a 2″ cookie cutter

Cal	Prot	Fat	Carb	Fiber	Chol	Sodium
180kc	2g	4.5g	35g	<1g	10mg	120mg

Grandma's Snickerdoodles

1 cup shortening
1½ cup sugar
2 eggs, beaten
2½ cups flour + 2 tblsp
2 tsp. cream of tartar
1 tsp. soda
½ tsp. salt
1 tsp. vanilla

Cream shortening, add sugar & eggs one at a time, beat until fluffy. Sift flour with cream of tartar, soda & salt, add to first mixture. Stir. Form into balls the size of walnuts, roll in mixture of 2 tblsp sugar, and 2 tsp cinnamon. Grease baking sheet.

Bake 400 degrees for 8–9 minutes.

Recipe from: Grandma Carrie Detar

Cal	Prot	Fat	Carb	Fiber	Chol	Sodium
60kc	1g	3g	7g	0g	5mg	35mg

Grandma's Snickerdoodles (Revised)

Cream shortening and 1½ cups sugar, add eggs one at a time, beat well after each addition, add vanilla. Combine flour, cream of tartar, baking soda and salt, gradually add to creamed mixture; beat until smooth. Chill 1 hour or more.

Preheat oven to 400 degrees; lightly spray cookie sheets with vegetable spray.

Combine remaining ¼ cup sugar and cinnamon; set aside. Form chilled dough into balls the size of walnuts; roll balls of dough in cinnamon-sugar mixture. Place balls on prepared cookie sheets. Bake in a 400-degree oven for 8–9 minutes.

vegetable spray
1 cup margarine
1¾ cups sugar, divided
1 egg + 2 egg whites, beaten
1 teaspoon vanilla extract
2½ cup + 2 tablespoons
    all-purpose flour
2 teaspoon cream of tartar
1 teaspoon baking soda
dash salt
2 teaspoons cinnamon

Yield: 78 cookies

Cal	Prot	Fat	Carb	Fiber	Chol	Sodium
60kc	1g	2.5g	8g	0g	0mg	50mg

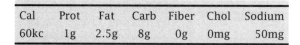

his recipe came from a dear friend in Ohio who is also a terrific cook. Since our oldest grandchild, Joe, has been big enough to stand on a stool at the cabinet the grandchildren have all helped me make cookies; Jenny, John, Andy, Clay, and Sara especially like to decorate them. When I ask what kind they want to make they say without fail, "Nana's sugar cookies."

Betty's Sugar Cookies

1 cup margarine
1 egg
1&½ cup sifted
   powdered sugar
1 tsp vanilla
2&½ cup flour
1 tsp. baking powder
¼ tsp. salt
1 tsp. cream of tartar

Mix all together, refrigerate about one hour. Roll out on floured countertop, cut out. Put on ungreased cookie pan. Bake 400 degrees until edges turn brown about 7–8 minutes.

Recipe from: Betty Mougey

Cal	Prot	Fat	Carb	Fiber	Chol	Sodium
70kc	1g	4g	8g	0g	5mg	75mg

Nana's Sugar Cookies (Revised)

This has become a favorite with all our grandchildren, and they always want to help me make them, which explains the change in the name.

Cream margarine and sugar, add egg and vanilla; beat well. Combine flour, baking powder, salt, and cream of tartar. Gradually add to creamed mixture, stir well. Cover and refrigerate at least one hour. Preheat oven to 400 degrees; very lightly spray cookie sheets with vegetable spray. Spoon portions of dough onto lightly floured countertop, roll until about ¼" thick. Cut with cookie cutter, place on prepared cookie sheets and sprinkle with sugar or sprinkles. Bake at 400 degrees about 7–8 minutes or until edges turn golden.

¾ cup margarine
1½ cup powdered sugar
1 egg, slightly beaten
1 teaspoon vanilla extract
2½ cup flour
1 teaspoon baking powder
dash salt
1 teaspoon cream of tartar
decorative sugar or sprinkles

Yield: 48 cookies

Cal	Prot	Fat	Carb	Fiber	Chol	Sodium
70kc	1g	3g	9g	0g	5mg	50mg

Desserts

Drop Sugar Cookies

Sift together:
2½ cups sifted flour
½ teaspoon cream of tartar
½ tsp soda
¾ tsp salt

Cream together:
½ cup butter
1 cup sugar
1 tsp milk
add 1 egg

Cream till fluffy. Stir in dry ingredients, until mixture is smooth. Blend in 2 tlb milk. Drop by tsp on cookie sheet. Flatten with bottom of water glass dipped in sugar. Bake 400 oven 12 min.

Recipe from: Caroline Shriver

Cal	Prot	Fat	Carb	Fiber	Chol	Sodium
50kc	1g	2g	8g	0g	10mg	65mg

Drop Sugar Cookies (Revised)

Preheat oven to 375 degrees; spray cookie sheets with vegetable spray. Combine flour, baking soda, cream of tartar and salt in a small bowl. In a large mixing bowl cream margarine and sugar until fluffy; add milk, egg, vanilla and almond extract. Gradually add dry ingredients, beating until mixture is smooth. Chill at least one hour. Roll into balls the size of walnuts then roll in additional sugar. Rub a small amount of margarine on bottom of water glass, then dip in sugar, gently slightly flatten each cookie, dipping into sugar after each cookie. Bake 9–10 minutes in 375 degree oven.

Yield: 54 cookies

2½ cups all-purpose flour
½ teaspoon baking soda
½ teaspoon cream of tartar
¼ teaspoon salt
½ cup margarine
1 cup sugar
2 tablespoons reduced-fat milk
1 egg
2 teaspoons vanilla extract
½ teaspoon almond extract

Cal	Prot	Fat	Carb	Fiber	Chol	Sodium
50kc	1g	2g	8g	0g	5mg	45mg

FROZEN DESSERTS

Jean's Sherbet

1 large can milk
1 quart milk
1¾ cup sugar
2 eggs, beaten
1 large can crushed pineapple
1 tsp vanilla
1 bottle cherries

Combine all ingredients, pour into shallow pans; place in freezer of refrigerator, turn temperature on high, when partly frozen turn down.

Recipe from: Jean Detar

Cal	Prot	Fat	Carb	Fiber	Chol	Sodium
160kc	3g	3.5g	32g	0g	30mg	45mg

Jean's Sherbet (Revised)

Combine all ingredients, pour into shallow pans; place in freezer for at least 24 hours.

Remove from freezer about 15 minutes before serving.

Yield: 20 servings

1-(12 oz.) can skim
   evaporated milk
1 quart reduced-fat milk
1½ cups sugar
½ cup egg substitute
1-(20 oz.) can crushed
   pineapple
1 teaspoon vanilla
1 cup maraschino cherries

Cal	Prot	Fat	Carb	Fiber	Chol	Sodium
130kc	4g	1g	28g	0g	5mg	60mg

Rice Chex Ice Cream

¾ cups Rice Chex
½ cup moist coconut
1½ cup light brown sugar
¾ cups chopped pecans
¾ cup butter

Pour melted butter over ingredients. Spread half into oblong cake pan, soften or slice ½ gallon vanilla ice cream and put over mixture. Cover with balance of rice chex mixture. Put in freezer over nite, (sic).

Recipe from: Caroline Shriver

Cal	Prot	Fat	Carb	Fiber	Chol	Sodium
360kc	3g	22g	41g	<1g	55mg	170mg

Rice Chex Ice Cream (Revised)

Place cereal, coconut, sugar, and nuts in a bowl; pour melted margarine over all; stir. Spread half into a 9×13 pan; slice or spoon softened vanilla ice cream, place on top of cereal mixture. Cover with remaining cereal mixture. Cover; freeze at least overnight. This will stay good for several days.

Yield: 15 servings

¾ cups Rice or Corn Chex
⅓ cup moist coconut
1⅓ cups light brown sugar
¼ cups chopped pecans
⅓ cup margarine, melted
½ gallon vanilla reduced-fat
     ice cream, ice milk or
     frozen dessert

Cal	Prot	Fat	Carb	Fiber	Chol	Sodium
230kc	3g	9g	37g	0g	10mg	135mg

Cherry Cream Freeze

1 can Eagle Brand milk
¼ cup lemon juice
2 ½ cups cherry pie filling
¾ cup crushed pineapple
¼ tsp almond extract
2 cups whipped cream

Combine first 5 ingredients and fold in whipped cream. Freeze in 9×5×3 pan. Freeze for 25 hours.

Cal	Prot	Fat	Carb	Fiber	Chol	Sodium
260kc	3g	14g	30g	0g	50mg	55mg

Cherry Cream Freeze (Revised)

Combine first 5 ingredients and fold in whipped topping. Pour into a 10×6 or similar size pan. Freeze overnight, remove from freezer about 10 minutes before serving.

Yield: fifteen 2″ square servings

1 (14 oz.) can fat-free
    sweetened condensed milk
¼ cup lemon juice
1 (21 oz.) can cherry pie filling
1 (15 oz.) can crushed
    pineapple, partially drained
¼ teaspoon almond flavoring
2 cups reduced-fat nondairy
    whipped topping

Cal	Prot	Fat	Carb	Fiber	Chol	Sodium
160kc	3g	1g	33g	0g	0mg	40mg

Desserts

MISCELLANEOUS DESSERTS

Mom's Fruit Rings

Fruit Rings were another favorite of the Shriver family. Mom Shriver would make them with peaches in the summer and apples in the fall. She served them in a bowl with milk to pour over them; I prefer to have a scoop of vanilla ice cream over the hot rings.

1 cup sugar
1 cup water
Boil just to dissolve.
2¼ cup Bisquick
⅔ cup milk
fruit, (apples or peaches),
    peeled & chopped fine.
2 tblsp. butter

Make biscuit dough from Bisquick. Pour syrup in casserole dish. Roll dough out; spread unsweetened fruit over dough. Roll up and slice about 1″ thick. Lay cut side up in syrup. Dot with butter, sprinkle with cinnamon. Bake in 350° oven for 45 minutes.

Recipe from: Eleanor Shriver

Cal	Prot	Fat	Carb	Fiber	Chol	Sodium
120kc	1g	3.5g	21g	0g	5mg	190mg

Mom's Fruit Rings (Revised)

Combine sugar and water; boil until dissolved, pour into a 10×10″ or 9×13″ baking dish. For ease in rolling soft dough, I sprinkle countertop lightly with a little water, place a sheet of waxed paper on wet surface. (The water holds it in place.) Sprinkle with flour.

Combine baking mix and milk with a fork, scrape out onto floured surface; roll about ¼″ thick. Spread prepared fruit over dough. Roll up like a jellyroll and slice about 1″ thick. Place slices, cut side up, in syrup, sprinkle with cinnamon. Bake in 350° oven for 45 minutes or until nicely browned and bubbly.

1½ cup sugar
1½ cup water
2¼ cup reduced-fat baking
    mix
⅔ cup reduced-fat milk
2½ cups fruit, peeled and
    chopped fine.
cinnamon

Yield: 20 servings

Cal	Prot	Fat	Carb	Fiber	Chol	Sodium
120kc	1g	1g	27g	<1g	0mg	160mg

Summer Delight

1 large pkg. strawberry Jell-O
2 cups boiling water
large pkg. frozen strawberries
½-cup cold water
1 loaf size angel food cake or
   ¾ of round cake
2 small pkg. instant coconut
   pudding
3 cups cold milk
2 cups Cool Whip
3 ½ oz. shredded coconut
½-cup walnuts, chopped
bananas

Dissolve the Jell-O in boiling water, add strawberries and cold water; pour into 9×13 pan. Tear cake into bite size pieces and soak in Jell-O; refrigerate. Mix pudding according to directions but omitting 1 cup milk, spread over Jell-O; refrigerate. Spread whipped topping over pudding, sprinkle with coconut and nuts. Cut into squares; put banana slices on top.

Recipe from: Brenda Shriver

Cal	Prot	Fat	Carb	Fiber	Chol	Sodium
210kc	4g	6g	35g	1g	5mg	300mg

Summer Delight (Revised)

Dissolve the Jell-O in boiling water, add strawberries and cold water; stir until thawed, pour into 9×13 pan. Tear cake into bite size pieces,add to Jell-O, set aside until cake has absorbed Jell-O; refrigerate until firm. Mix pudding with milk, stir in coconut flavoring. Spread pudding over Jell-O/cake; refrigerate until set. Spread whipped topping over pudding, sprinkle with coconut and nuts. When ready to serve: Cut into squares place on individual serving plate, garnish with banana slices.

Yield: 20 servings

*If not available use vanilla pudding and add 1 teaspoon coconut flavoring

1 (6 oz) pkg. strawberry Jell-O
2 cups boiling water
20 oz. pkg. frozen strawberries
½ cup cold water
1 loaf size angel food cake or
   ¾ of round cake
2 (3½ oz) pkg. fat-free vanilla
   pudding*
3 cups reduced-fat milk
1 teaspoon coconut flavoring
2 cups reduced-fat non-dairy
   whipped topping
½ cup shredded coconut
¼ cup walnuts, chopped
bananas

Cal	Prot	Fat	Carb	Fiber	Chol	Sodium
170kc	3g	3g	34g	1g	0mg	320mg

Desserts

Beverages

I enjoy iced tea year round. However, I will admit that there is nothing quite as refreshing on a hot summer day as a tall, cold glass of mint tea.

Mint Tea

2 cups boiling water
2 family size tea bags**
3 sprigs fresh mint;
1 cup sugar*
3–4 cups cold water
2 tablespoons lemon juice

Add tea bags to water, let steep 5–8 minutes. Add remaining ingredients, serve over ice.

Yield: 4 servings

*Can substitute ⅛ cup sugar and 1½ teaspoons powdered artificial sweetener.

Cal	Prot	Fat	Carb	Fiber	Chol	Sodium
190kc	0g	0g	51g	0g	0mg	10mg

Momma's Sweetened Iced Tea

Bring 6 cups water to a boil, add tea bags, reduce heat and simmer for 1 minute. Remove from heat, cover and let steep about 10 minutes. Add sugar to hot tea and stir until dissolved. Put about 3 cups of ice cubes in a 1 gallon pitcher, pour hot tea over ice cubes, add enough cold water to fill the pitcher or until desired strength.

Serve over ice with a lemon slice.

Yield: sixteen 2-cup servings

Recipe from: Oma Day

water
4 family size tea bags**
1 cup sugar
ice cubes
lemon slices

Cal	Prot	Fat	Carb	Fiber	Chol	Sodium
50kc	0g	0g	13g	0g	0mg	4mg

Sun Tea

Put 5 family size tea bags** in 1 gallon water. Let stand in hot sun for several hours, until tea is fairly dark. DO NOT DILUTE. Sweeten as desired.

Yield: 11 servings

Cal	Prot	Fat	Carb	Fiber	Chol	Sodium
0kc	0g	0g	0g	0g	0mg	10mg

Microwave Tea

2 family size tea bags** in 2 cups water, microwave on high for 4 minutes. Cover and let steep for 5 minutes. Add 2–3 cups cold water to dilute.

To sweeten add 1 cup sugar or ⅛ cup sugar and 1½ teaspoons artificial sweetener.

Yield: 4 servings

Recipe from: Judy Morris

Cal	Prot	Fat	Carb	Fiber	Chol	Sodium
190kc	0g	0g	50g	0g	0mg	7mg

Fruited Mint Tea

3 cups boiling water
1 family size tea bag**
12 fresh mint sprigs
1 cup sugar
¼ cup lemon juice
1 cup orange juice
5 cups water

Pour boiling water over tea bags and mint; cover and steep 5 minutes. Remove tea bags and mint. Add remaining ingredients.

Yield: 7 servings

*Can substitute ⅛ cup sugar and 1½ teaspoons artificial sweetener.
**1 family size tea bag is the equivalent of 3 or 4 regular size tea bags.

Cal	Prot	Fat	Carb	Fiber	Chol	Sodium
130kc	1g	0g	34g	0g	0mg	10mg

Hot Spiced Cider

Place cinnamon sticks and cloves in cheesecloth; tie in knot. Place cider in large kettle, add remaining ingredients, and place over medium heat until hot. Remove cheesecloth bag and discard. Serve hot or cold over ice.

Recipe from: Brookfield Garden Club

2 quarts apple cider
½ cup brown sugar, packed
three 3-inch cinnamon sticks
dash nutmeg
½–1 teaspoon ground cinnamon, according to taste
1 teaspoon whole cloves

Cal	Prot	Fat	Carb	Fiber	Chol	Sodium
166kc	0g	.4g	41g	<1g	0mg	23mg

Beverages

Hot Wassail Mix

2 cups Tang drink mix
one 3-oz. package presweetened
    lemonade powder
1½ cup sugar
1 teaspoon cinnamon
½ teaspoon ground cloves

Mix all ingredients thoroughly, place in airtight container until ready for use.

To serve: Add 2–3 teaspoons of dry mix to 1 cup hot water; stir well.

Yield: 3½ cups dry mix or 56 servings

Cal	Prot	Fat	Carb	Fiber	Chol	Sodium
60kc	0g	0g	14g	0g	0mg	0mg

Punch for a Bunch

In a large mixing bowl dissolve Jell-O in boiling water; add remaining ingredients except ginger ale. Distribute liquids evenly among 4 containers and freeze. Remove from freezer and place in a punch bowl a few minutes before serving, add ginger ale and serve immediately.

Yield: thirty-eight 6-ounce servings

Recipe from: Colleyville Garden Club

two 6 oz. pkg. apricot Jell-O
1 cup boiling water
3 cup water
one 12 oz. can frozen
    lemonade, undiluted
one 46 oz. can apricot nectar
one 46 oz. can pineapple juice
2 quarts cold water
4 quarts cold ginger ale

Cal	Prot	Fat	Carb	Fiber	Chol	Sodium
120kc	1g	0g	31g	0g	0mg	30mg

Pickles and Preserves

Sara's Apple Butter

18 cups apple sauce,
    preferably home made
9 cups sugar
1 cup cider vinegar
2–3 teaspoon cinnamon
1 teaspoon ground cloves
¼ teaspoon allspice

Put all ingredients in oven at 350 degrees in enamel roaster. Cover with lid while in oven, cook for 3½ hours, stirring every 15 minutes. (Pack in sterilized canning jars; follow manufacturer's directions.)

Yield: 6 pints

Recipe from: Sara Darr

Cal	Prot	Fat	Carb	Fiber	Chol	Sodium
1485kc	1g	.5g	386g	9g	0mg	19mg

Sue's Peach Preserves

Bring to boil and boil 20 minutes, set off (heat) and stir in 1 small box of orange lime; stir until dissolved and put in jars.*

Follow canning jar manufacturer's directions.

6 cups diced peaches
2 cups crushed pineapple
8 cups sugar

Yield: 5½ pints

Recipe from: Sue Roselle

Cal	Prot	Fat	Carb	Fiber	Chol	Sodium
1382kc	1g	0g	356g	5g	0mg	11mg

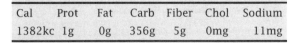

Pickles & Preserves

Quick Dill Pickles

3 quarts water

1 quart white vinegar

1 cup pickling salt (not iodized) Mix
    and bring to boil.

1 head fresh dill for each quart

1 small clove garlic for each quart

1 tsp mustard seed for each quart

6–8 peppercorns for each quart

¼ tsp powdered alum for each
    quart

1 pod hot pepper or ¼ tsp ground
    red pepper for each quart

Scrub cucumbers, put head of dill in each qt. jar, then pack cucumbers tightly in jar, add remaining ingredients to each jar. Place jars in shallow pan of boiling water and fill jars with boiling brine mixture. Wipe jar mouths clean & seal. Leave jars in hot water for 10–15 minutes.* Make sure all lids seal; store for 6 weeks before using. These are delicious & easy to make.

Yield: 8–10 quarts

Recipe from: Joy Walker

*Follow canning jar manufacturer's directions.

Cal	Prot	Fat	Carb	Fiber	Chol	Sodium
329kc	1g	.5g	81g	81g	0mg	9159mg

hile living in Tucson, Arizona, I had the privilege of becoming friends with Ann and Harry Capen, retired missionaries. Ann and Harry had gone to Africa in the 1920s, where they served for fifty years, sharing God's Word with the African people. We loved to gather around and listen to them talk about their days "in the mission field." I can't imagine what conditions would have been like trying to raise a family there, but I know Ann and Harry felt greatly blessed to have been chosen by God to serve in this way. Ann was certainly an inspiration to anyone who ever met her and a delightful person to be around.

Ann's Seven Day Sweet Pickles

This is a 7-day process. Yes, it is a little more trouble, but once you taste the pickles you'll agree it was time well spent.

7 lb. smallish cucumbers

boiling water to cover cucumbers

1 qt vinegar

6½ cups sugar (or less)

2 tblsp salt

2 tblsp mixed pickle spices (tie in
    cheesecloth)

Wash cucumbers, place in heavy mixing bowl or crock; cover with boiling water. Place a dinner plate over all. Let stand 24 hours; drain, rinse each cucumber and put back in crock, pour more boiling water over to cover. Continue to repeat this for 4 days using fresh water each time and rinsing the cucumbers. On the 5th day; cut cucumbers into ¼″ slices or cut lengthwise. Combine vinegar, sugar, salt and spices, bring to a boil and pour over sliced cucumbers. On 6th day, drain syrup into pan and bring to a boil, pour over cucumbers. On the 7th day; drain off the syrup again into a large pan, add cucumber slices and bring to a boiling point. DO NOT BOIL CUCUMBERS. Pack hot cucumbers and syrup into sterilized, hot jars, seal.* Set aside to cool and make sure each lid has sealed. If some do not seal, store in refrigerator and use first. (This is a lot of fuss, but I think they are the best sweet pickles I've ever eaten, I make them when I have the opportunity.)

Yield: 8–9 pints

Recipe from: Ann Capen

*Follow canning jars manufacturer's directions.

Cal	Prot	Fat	Carb	Fiber	Chol	Sodium
616kc	2g	.5g	159g	2g	0mg	1560mg

Caring for Your Cast Iron Cookware

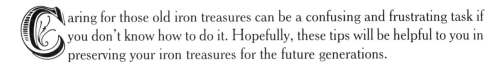 aring for those old iron treasures can be a confusing and frustrating task if you don't know how to do it. Hopefully, these tips will be helpful to you in preserving your iron treasures for the future generations.

1. Clean immediately after using. If you can, simply wipe out with paper towel, if necessary, wash with mild soap.

2. Do not wash in a dishwasher or use harsh soaps.

3. After washing, dry completely. I leave mine set out for a few minutes before storing. Store with a paper towel between skillets and NEVER store with the lid on because they need air circulating around them.

4. Never use sharp tools to scrape burned food off skillet, add a small amount of water, return to heat and let simmer for a few minutes to loosen burned-on food.

5. If you get a grease build-up, clean with steel wool pad, then reseason.

6. To season your skillets, pour vegetable oil into the skillet; then, using a soft cloth, coat the entire surface top and bottom with the oil. Preheat oven to 350 degrees, place skillet in hot oven for about one hour. Turn off the oven, but do not remove the skillet until oven has cooled. Some people like to turn the skillet upside down while doing this.

7. If you cook tomatoes, or any acidic food or beans in your iron skillets, after cleaning well, either season again or coat the inside with a nonstick vegetable spray and wipe well with paper towel.

8   To remove rust from a skillet, you can scrub with a wire bristle brush or steel wool pad to remove rust; wash and season again. If the skillet looks hopeless, take it to a place that will sandblast it for you, then all you have to do is season before you use it again.

Index

Index

Index

Index